Soul Mate Dolls

Noreen Crone-Findlay

Krause Publications
700 E. State St.
Iola, WI 54990-0001
715-445-2214
www.krause.com

Please call or write for our free catalog of publications. Our toll-free number to
place an order or obtain a free catalog is 800-258-0929 or please use our regular
business telephone 715-445-2214 for editorial comment and further information.

Library of Congress Catalog Number 99-66140
ISBN 0-87341-806-9

Some products in this book are registered trademarks of their respective companies:
Friendly Looms, Lap Loom A™
Igolochkoy™
Weavette Looms™

Photos by Judy Wood and Noreen Crone-Findlay. Back cover author photo by Jim Findlay.

dedication

This book is lovingly dedicated to the center of my universe: my husband, Jim Findlay, our daughter, Chloë, and our son, Angus. The three of you bring me unbelievable joy. Without you, this book could not have happened.

acknowledgments

So many things and so many people have come together to support the creation of this book. I am eternally grateful to all of them, and so pleased to be able to say "Thank you!" now.

First of all, I want to start by thanking *you* for joining me on this journey. I may not know your name, but I did write this book for you.

The older I get, the more I appreciate nature, especially the trees and all they give us. I want to thank the trees who became the paper for this book.

One of the great joys in building this book has been the pleasure of working with special people. My most enormous gratitude goes to:

Michele McKenzie, the Creative Manager at Bernat/Spinrite, for introducing my work to Krause Publications, and for being a Fairy Godmother in general.

Mary Jo Kewley, Acquisitions Editor at Krause, for her creative vision in seeing the potential of this book, and of course, to Amy Tincher-Durik, my Editor/Project Manager extraordinaire. Also, thank you to Jan Wojtech who designed these pages. While I'm at it, thank you all at Krause Publications. What a neat company.

I am blessed with having some wonderful friends. There were a few in particular who were exceptionally supportive and nurturing during the creation of this book, especially: Ardis Johnson, Dr. William Ramer, Brenda and Bob Bear, Arlee Hoiness, Terri Christiansen, and Bonnie Magee. I just can't thank you enough for your loving kindness.

A very large thank you to the suppliers of wonderful tools and materials for the book, and the special people who represent those treasures:

Bernat/Spinrite Yarns

Jules and Kaethe Kliot at Lacis

Mark Williams, Director of Retail at Lee Valley Tools

Lauri Hanna at Harrisville Designs

Lois Caron at The Caron Collection

Gail and Richard Bird at Birdhouse Enterprises

Thank you, Judy Wood, for the photographs, the great suggestions, and for hanging in there in the incredibly arduous process of photographing the book. Whew!

We were blessed in the photo sessions by my darling cat, Minnaloushe. She decided to model for us and added special moments and some much needed laughter. Judy and I thought that we might need to add a clause saying "No animals were harmed in this production!"

Thank you to Tarra Kongsrude for suggesting that I design a Millennium Doll.

Thank you, Susan Draper, for inspiring the Doll of All Possibilities, the Seed Child Soul Mate Doll.

Thank you to Brenda and Stephanie Bear for inspiring the Pah Shaw Doll.

Thank you, Terri Rambold, for seeing that the image of the carved door *had* to go back into the book, after I had taken it out.

Thank you, Dr. Christiane Northrup, for your kind words of encouragement. They came when I really needed them. And thank you so much for the inspiring work you do.

I am really grateful to all of the people who have participated in my workshops. I am fascinated by the way people learn, and in reaching to find new ways of enhancing that experience, I always learn so much myself. I love creating the workshops and I love what you bring to them. I have learned so much from all of you. Thank you!

Last, but most emphatically not least, great thanks to my totally wonderful family: my husband, Jim Findlay, thanks Honey, for all of the love and techno help; our daughter, Chloë Crone-Findlay, thanks for all of the design consultations and delicious meals; and our son, Angus Findlay, also a super techno helper. Thank you three for the love, support, and tenderness, as well as the raunchy humor! You three are the sun, moon, and stars to me.

Thanks to Aleksa Harkness and Patricia Heeren for being sisters, and not just in-laws, and for their enthusiastic support. Thanks to my other Mum, "Amazing Grace" Findlay, for her love and cheering-on.

Writing this book has required long hours and intense focus and has made some sacrifices necessary. One of those was that I was unable to help my Mom and Dad, Doris and Ray Crone, move from one city to another. Thank you, so much, Mom, for saying, "Don't come!" Thank you so much to my brothers, David and Jonathan Crone, and especially my sister, Dr. Lesley-Ann Crone, for being there and doing it all. (And Uncle Gene and Auntie June Grimes—bless your hearts!)

I feel enormous gratitude and appreciation to and for our entire circle of loved ones. So much to be grateful for…

table of contents

introduction

Human beings have an amazing ability to heal themselves, physically, emotionally, and spiritually. When there is a wound in the heart or soul, a wonderful way to heal it is to find a soul mate and embark on a journey of creativity. Simply having fun while questing for depth and meaning can add untold zest and joy to living. That's what this book is all about: playing with images and metaphors, while paying attention to how the processes work on a deeper level. It is intended to inspire feelings of wholeness, not to be seen as medical or therapeutic advice.

I love teaching people how to use the magical art of dollmaking to inspire, heal, and delight themselves. In my workshops, they learn how to make dolls that are like very special friends of the heart and imagination. That's why I call this process Soul Mate Dollmaking.

In Soul Mate Dollmaking, we work with many kinds of tools. There are the concrete tools like paper, pens, and scissors, but then there are also abstract concepts, which may seem odd in a book about dollmaking. We use the abstract tools to deepen the connection between the heart and hands.

One of the most important abstract tools we'll pay attention to is metaphor. Metaphors create pictures with words. On a deeper level, they build bridges by forming connections that can illuminate and enlighten us. They help us turn stumbling blocks into stepping stones.

Working mindfully with our hands somehow reaches deep into our souls. In making very special objects, like dolls, we can engage our minds at a mythical level and heal our hearts.

Here's an example of how Soul Mate Dollmaking works. We'll start with a conversation:

I was talking to a dear friend, Brenda, about people who can "put your light out" with their squelching ways.

With her ancient 11-year-old wisdom, Brenda's daughter, Stephanie, sighed and said, "You two need to learn to fight like a GIRL!"

"Huh?"

"First, you roll your eyes, then, take a deep breath and your shoulder goes up, like this… Now, bend your arm, flick your wrist, swish off their nastiness, and say, really loudly: 'PAH SHAW!!!!' Then you strut away with your head held way up high! They'll be surprised and it will make you laugh!"

We tried it. We liked it. She was right.

The next step was to design and make a Soul Mate Doll that would deepen the experience. Her job is to remind me about the pleasures of delivering a hearty "Pah Shaw!" when one is called for. You might enjoy having one in your life! (At the end of Chapter 1, there are instructions for the Pah Shaw Soul Mate Doll.)

So, the Soul Mate Dollmaking process is:

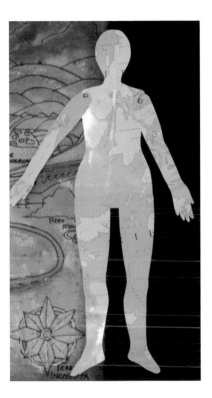

1. Recognize a need. (Ouch, those squelchers!) This can just as easily be a positive experience that you wish to celebrate, embody, and remember.
2. Find something that heals that need ("Pah Shaw!") (or celebrates something special).
3. Make a doll that embodies that healing or celebration. Enjoy the physical and emotional pleasures of making the doll.
4. See the doll and remember its meaning. Live that meaning!

This book is a potpourri of techniques for you to sample and use as a launching pad for your own creativity. I really encourage you to try techniques that are new to you. I've designed the projects to be at a fairly "entry" level to entice you to explore them.

The "directions" or "instructions" are intended as suggestions or recipes. Soul Mate Dollmaking is very much like creative cooking—recipes are personal things, and each is enhanced by a pinch of that and touch of this each cook brings to it. I will explain to you how I've made each Soul Mate Doll, but feel free to do it in your own way.

You may see a doll in the book that really sings to you. Go ahead and make it, whether or not the associated process resonates with you. What I call one thing may trigger a totally different response in you.

So, let's go play dollies!

Noreen Crone - Findlay

(One word of caution: Please do not give Soul Mate Dolls to young children. Most of them are not designed for little ones.)

1 chapter

The Basic Flat Soul Mate Doll

Some Basic Flat Soul Mate Dolls, made in varying sizes.

I've been teaching workshops on creativity and dollmaking for many years. So many of my students have expressed anxiety and frustration about "not being able to make anything/to sew/to draw/to get over their stumbling blocks" that I had to come up with a way of dollmaking that would launch them past those blockages.

In response, I've developed a process of dollmaking that I call Basic Flat Soul Mate Dolls.

Flat dolls are a really great way to begin Soul Mate Dollmaking. They are quite simple to make, adaptable and accessible, and can be totally "no-sew." Flat dolls are like paper dolls with chutzpah: they are sturdy (so they can have great adventures), dressable (oh, yes!), and have moveable joints (don't we all need to be flexible?).

Soul Mate Dolls are ambassadors from the realm of imagination, so we begin with imagination...

A Guided Visualization: The Magical Garden

We are going to begin by going on a journey—a journey to meet a special friend who is going to give you your first Soul Mate Doll. You may wish to tape this for yourself or have a friend read it to you.

Book some time to nurture yourself, and turn off as much of the outside world as you can. Make yourself very comfortable. Close your eyes. Breathe in and let the air move through you, bringing feelings of safety, comfort, and ease.

When you are ready, imagine that you are looking down. Notice that a path is at your feet. It is a very inviting path, just the right width, bordered by flowers and trees. The air is soft. Birds are singing. The air smells sweet and clean. The path invites you to move forward.

Follow the path until you come to a beautiful, ancient stone wall. The stones in the wall are warm in the sunlight. The wall is quite high and goes as far as the eye can see in both directions. It encloses a garden.

There is a hidden doorway. Even though the door is massive, it opens, smoothly, welcoming you into the garden. You go in, locking the door behind you.

Follow the path to a clearing. In the center of the clearing, there is a bench. You see that there is someone, a friend, sitting on the bench. You are filled with delight at recognizing this person (even if you have never met him/her in your "real" life) and you go to him or her, without hesitation.

Your friend is really happy to see you, and says, "I have something for you," and hands you a parcel that is wrapped in a special way. Taking your time, you savor the unwrapping. It is a very special Flat Doll—your first Soul Mate Doll. This is a doll that you have longed for, perhaps without even knowing it.

You study the doll very closely, feeling her textures, weight, noting her colors, her shapes, the expression on her face, and observing her hands. She is uniquely yours and may surprise you in the way materials are used. You memorize everything about her, knowing that you will remember her and be able to make her when you leave the garden. You thank your friend and say goodbye, agreeing to meet again.

When you are ready, in your own time and your own way, you come back here. Remember, you can return to your garden any time to be refreshed and renewed. Write down everything you can remember about your doll. What was her body like? Was she short, tall, thin, plump? Did you see her feet? Was she human, mythical, or animal? Did she have wings or a mermaid's tail? How old was she? What color was her hair? What was she wearing? Did she have any jewelry or other special objects or tools with her? Was there anything in her hands? What colors were her clothes? What were the textures of her garments? What did she have on her feet? What was the most noticeable thing about her? Was there a suggestion of a time frame or place about her?

If the answers to these questions aren't clear, close your eyes, take a deep breath, and imagine yourself back in the garden. Imagine that you are holding her in your hands, looking for the answers to these questions. Let yourself "just make it up" if the images are unclear. Now it's time to make her:

Materials and Tools

There are some basic materials and tools that are used in making all of the Flat Soul Mate Dolls in the book. (Some of the dolls require special tools. These will be listed in the instructions for that specific doll.) The basic materials and tools are:

- Awl
- Black fine-point permanent marker or black ink and pen
- Card stock: You'll become a champion "re-claimer," questing for useful pieces of card stock. The best ones don't have printing on them, because the printing on boxes can keep glue from working. Some of the larger dolls need to be made in heavier weight card stock, so for them, I glue two layers of card stock together. For folded or small dolls, lightweight card stock is fine. I really like four-

ply card stock I buy at my local art supply store. I don't like mat board, because it separates easily and doesn't stand up well to dollmaking. Corrugated cardboard works well for the chairs on page 46. Regular corrugated cardboard is not suitable for most of the Soul Mate Dolls, although I have found some that has much narrower corrugations and is quite thin. It has a charm of its own and is quite acceptable.

🦃 Colored pencils, crayons, or paint
🦃 Craft knife
🦃 Cutting mat (or a piece of scrap cardboard)
🦃 Darning needle
🦃 Decorative papers (including handmade, brown, origami, gift wrap, magazine photos, etc.): These are optional, for you can do what I do: decorate your own paper with paint, crayons, stamps, stencils, or markers.
🦃 Ephemera: Treasures that have accumulated and have sentimental value—the button from that special shirt, a bottle cap with a picture of a bee on it, a broken earring from your special auntie, tiny sea shells, beads, and so on—make great decorations for Soul Mate Dolls.
🦃 Glue (white and hot glue gun and sticks)
🦃 Needlenose pliers
🦃 Notebook
🦃 Paper clips or 1-1/2" lengths of 18-gauge wire for joints (I like plastic-coated paper clips for making joints because you can match the colors to the dolls).
🦃 Pencil and eraser
🦃 Plain and skin-tone paper

Soul Mate Dollmaking tools.

🦃 Ruler
🦃 Safety glasses
🦃 Scissors
🦃 Small clamps
🦃 Small pieces of lightweight fabric to make hinges for hips and knees
🦃 Templates: Templates for Basic Flat Soul Mate Dolls are really handy, because they speed the construction process up a lot. You'll be using this pattern in a number of different ways for different Soul Mate Dolls. The pattern for the Flat Soul Mate Doll is glued to sturdy sheet plastic, although strong card stock also works. It is then cut out and used like a tracer. (I reclaimed the plastic tops off drapery samples for my templates. I was also given some plastic file folders that worked well for template making.)
🦃 Vanishing ink or erasable marker

🦃 Wire snips
🦃 Yarn, ribbons, feathers, etc. for hair
🦃 And last, but not least, a box, bag, or basket to keep it all together

When I was in art school, my favorite professor always told us to use the very best materials, tools, and equipment we could. It makes sense because these are the flesh and bones of your work. With this in mind, I have searched for really pleasing tools and materials for Soul Mate Dolls, which are listed for each doll. I found suppliers willing to take mail orders so your location isn't a limitation (see Suppliers and Sources, page 144). I have also worked out ways of making Soul Mate Dolls and their accessories that are low-cost alternatives in case your budget is tight.

Constructing the Basic Flat Soul Mate Doll

1. The pattern

You may want to enlarge or reduce the pattern with a scanner or photocopier. The pattern is just a suggestion; feel free to alter the doll's proportions and make her fatter, thinner, shorter, taller—whatever it takes to make an appropriate body for your doll. She may be a completely abstract figure, so doodle until she feels right. When you are satisfied that you have all of her body parts right, make yourself a template of them.

If you choose to use the pattern in the book just as it is, you'll need to remember that ink from scanners or photocopiers can rub off. Any lines that you want to have on your doll will have to be re-drawn with a fine-point permanent black marker if you have photocopied drawings.

Tracing around templates.

2. Don't be intimidated by the face.

One of the best tools I have ever found for drawing faces is an erasable or vanishing ink marker, found in the notions section of fabric stores. You can draw and erase to your heart's content and never mess up the face the way a pencil eraser does.

With the erasable marker, draw a vertical line lightly down the center of the head. Now draw a horizontal line roughly at the middle of the head and two more lines that divide the space from the chin to the midline evenly. Draw two dots (for the pupils) on the midline where the eyes will be. The size and shape of the eyes will determine the age of the doll. Youth is indicated by large eyes, slightly lower than the midline. An older face has eyes that are higher, smaller, and closer together. Play with different shapes of features; for example, the nose gets longer and thinner as the face ages. If she is wearing earrings, you might want to add ears to the sides of the head. The bottom of the ears are usually in a line with the end of the nose. When you are happy with the face, draw it in with permanent ink and shade with colored pencils.

The template face is looking

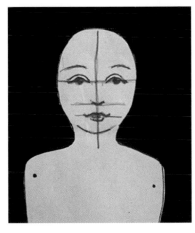

Sketching the face with the vanishing marker.

straight forward, but your Soul Mate Doll may have her head turned to one side with her face in profile (like the Millennium or Determined dolls, pages 118 and 111, respectively)—remember, this is your Soul Mate Doll, and you have complete permission to make her just the way she needs to be. I leave the face on my templates blank and draw it in on the individual dolls.

3. Glue the pattern or trace the templates onto the card stock.

If you don't like the color of your card stock, glue a pleasing shade of paper to one side of the card stock and your copied pattern to the other side. If your card stock is a pleasing shade, then simply trace around the templates.

4. Cut out your doll's body, arms, and legs.

I will often separate the individual parts of the doll body from the card stock with scissors. I prefer to do the "fine cutting" on the Soul Mate Doll with my craft knife. This avoids stressing the card stock at tricky turning points, such as chins and ankles.

Remember to always keep your "hold down" fingers out of the "slicing" line of the cutting edge. Also, for the sake of your tables, use a cutting mat, or put scrap cardboard under your project.

When cutting, always cut in light strokes, never putting too much pressure on the blade. It usually takes a few strokes to cut all of the way through the card stock. You might need to flip the piece over and run the knife along the back side of the

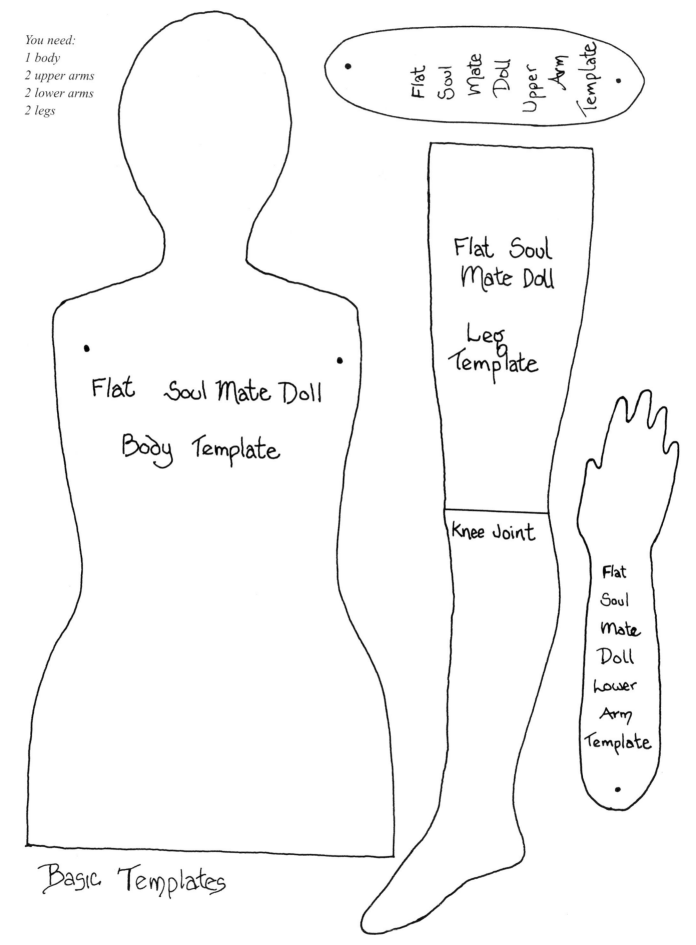

You need:
1 body
2 upper arms
2 lower arms
2 legs

Flat Soul Mate Doll Upper Arm Template

Flat Soul Mate Doll Body Template

Flat Soul Mate Doll Leg Template

Knee Joint

Flat Soul Mate Doll Lower Arm Template

Basic Templates

cut to fully release the piece. There is less chance of the knife skidding and hurting you or your doll if you follow this practice. Also, keep in mind that a dull knife is a dangerous knife—it can skid and plunge into you or your projects!

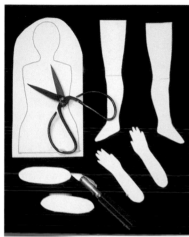

Cutting out the parts of the Basic Flat Soul Mate Doll.

5. Shoulder and elbow joints

Using an awl, pierce holes at the dots on the patterns. Lay the arm or body section on a cutting mat or scrap of cardboard. Push the awl down into the dot to get the hole started. This way you will avoid unintentionally piercing your fingers as well as the doll! If you don't have an awl (an incredibly handy tool) you can use a sharp darning needle (but an awl is so much better!).

For the joint loop, either cut 1-1/2" lengths of 18-gauge wire, or straighten out a paper clip, and cut it into two equal pieces. With needlenose pliers, bend one end of each piece into a small loop. Poke it through the hole in the shoulder on the body section, then through the hole in the upper arm. Bend the end of the wire into a loop, then fold over both loops and squeeze

both sides tightly with the pliers so there is a little resistance. Repeat for the other upper arm and for the elbow joint. The upper arm is placed under the lower arm before jointing.

Making the shoulder joints for the Basic Flat Soul Mate Doll.

6. Hip and knee joints

Cut two small rectangles of lightweight fabric, approximately 1" by 2" each. With the doll lying face up, place the thigh sections right up against the body's lower edge. Coat the fabric pieces with a thin layer of glue and place them so that half of the fabric piece is on the body and the other half is on the leg. Let dry thoroughly.

Cut across the line at the knee for the knee joint.

Turn the doll face down. Cut two more small pieces of fabric, approximately 3/4" by 2" for the knee joints. Place the lower leg snugly against the upper leg.

Coat the small fabric piece with a thin layer of glue and lay it on the leg, centering it over the knee joint. Let dry thoroughly.

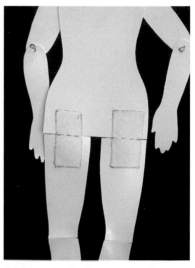

Making the thigh joints for the Basic Flat Soul Mate Doll.

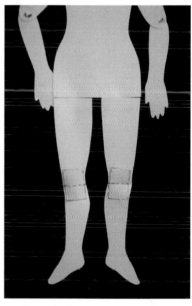

Making the knee joints for the Basic Flat Soul Mate Doll.

7. Optional

Color in or glue paper or fabric to the doll for stockings and underwear. Paint shoes on feet.

8. Hair

The hair can be drawn on and colored in before cutting out, or glued on afterwards.

Make tassels by wrapping yarn around one, two, three, or

four fingers, tying a knot at the top of the tassel and clipping the bottom. Hot-glue or sew it to the head, then clip and shape it.

Using tassels to make hair.

If you unravel strands from heavier weight yarn, it will give your doll wavy hair.

If her hair is swept up, you can make poofy-looking Edwardian styles by wrapping yarn around a length of cardboard, slipping it off the cardboard, and twisting it several times. Glue the twisted skein on, twirling and shaping it as you go.

You can make quite a wonderful hairstyle by taking a whole skein of embroidery floss, opening it up, twisting, and then gluing it to the doll's head.

Using skeins of embroidery floss (in this case, Kit Kin from Caron Threads) to make hair.

Skirts

Would your Flat Soul Mate Doll like to have a skirt?

A simple skirt is made by wrapping a ribbon around her waist, overlapping it by an inch or so, snipping it, and sewing a snap or hook and eye to the ends. Gather and sew a lightweight scarf or piece of fabric to the ribbon.

A simple skirt.

How about an even simpler skirt?

Take a bandanna-style handkerchief or head scarf and fold it in half. Cut a length of ribbon approximately 18" long. Slide it inside the fold. Gather the hanky along the fold and tie it around the doll's waist at the back. Make sure the gathers are evenly distributed around her waist.

A hanky skirt.

Lace Handkerchief Dress

Lay your doll on a 12" (approximate) square lace-trimmed hanky, face up. Have her arms stretched out horizontally. Bring the edges of the hanky to the front of the doll, crossing one slightly over the other. Lay a narrow 24" long ribbon just above the waist. Tie at the back and bring it over the shoulders to the front. Slip one end under the front ribbon. Tie a knot or bow. Arrange the hanky by folding the back upper edge down and the front upper corners down at an angle.

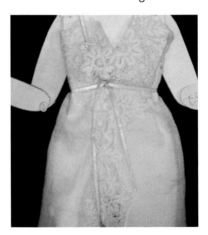

A ribbon holds the hanky dress together.

Basic Crocheted Hat

When you crochet this hat with a 4mm (G, 6) crochet hook and worsted weight "dishcloth" yarn (I used Lily Sugar'n Cream cotton), it will fit the Basic Flat Soul Mate Doll and the Serenity Doll (page 21). If you use a 3.5mm (E, 4) crochet hook and two strands of embroidery floss (two strands of regular "six-strand" embroidery floss, so technically, that's twelve single strands of floss) it will fit Great Aunt Gardener (page 130). This hat fit Great Aunt Gardener when I used Bernat's Cot'n Soft and a 3.5mm crochet hook. I also found that a "D" or 3.25mm crochet hook and Watercolours by Caron threads makes a wonderful hat for her. Crochet it with a 3.25mm (D, 3) crochet hook and one strand of embroidery floss (again, I am calling the undivided standard six-strand embroidery floss "one strand"), and it will fit Molly Whuppie (page 37).

Ch 3. Join to form ring.
1: Ch 1. 7 sc in ring.

Using different sized threads and yarns and appropriately sized crochet hooks will make different sized hats. They are all crocheted from the same pattern.

2: Ch 1. 2 sc in next 3 sc. 3 sc in next sc, 2 sc in next 3 sc. [15 sc]
3, 4, 5: Ch 1, 15 sc. Join.
6: Ch 3, dc in same sc. *3 dc in next sc, 2 dc in next sc*. Repeat from *-* to end of round. Join to ch 3. Cut yarn, weave in end.

Knitted Sweater

Here is a pattern, in plain knitting (Garter Stitch), for a cardigan for your Flat Soul Mate Doll. This fits the doll that is made from the unmodified pattern. If you changed the size of the doll pattern, you'll have to knit it on larger or smaller needles with appropriately sized yarn. The weight of yarn and needles you use will establish the size of the sweater.

Materials and Tools

Yarn (approx 2 oz.)*
Knitting needles*
Row counter
Darning needle
Scissors

The black-haired Basic Soul Mate Doll's sweater was knitted with 4.5mm knitting needles and Bernat Illusions #224 Waterfall-P.

Starting at the lower back:
Cast on 20 stitches.
Knit 2 rows plain.
R. 3: K 1 * yo, k 2 tog*. Repeat *-* across. Knit remaining st.
R. 4 - 30: Knit.
Begin the sleeves:
R. 31: Cast on 15 stitches at the beg. of row. Knit across.
R. 32: Cast on 15 stitches at beg. of this row. Knit across.
R. 33 - 47: (50 stitches) knit.
R. 48: K 20 st. Cast off 10 st. Knit remaining 20 st. Either

The Garter Stitch Sweater.

place the first 20 st. on a stitch holder, or ignore them for now, which is what I do.
R. 49 - 51: Knit these 20 stitches.
R. 52: Knit across, then cast on 5 st. at center.
R. 53-67: Knit these 25 st.
R. 68: Cast off 15 st. (completing the sleeve). K 10.
R. 69- 94: Knit these 10 st.
R. 95: K1 *yo, k 2 tog* 4x, k1.
R. 96-98: Knit across.
R. 99: Cast off.
Transfer stitches from stitch holder to needle. Attach yarn. Complete second half of front, reversing shaping. Sew side seams. Add any finishing touches your heart desires.

Crocheted Sweater

For those who prefer to crochet, here is a crocheted sweater for your Soul Mate Doll.

Materials and Tools

1 ball of yarn (approx 2 oz.)*
4.5mm crochet hook
5 small 1/4" buttons or 1/4" beads
Darning needle
Scissors

*Used in this project: (Partial ball of each) *Berella Muskoka color 9838, "Denims."*

Front: Make 1
Ch 18.
R. 1: 1 sc in 2nd ch from hook, 1 sc in each ch. [17 sc].
R. 2 - 12: Ch 1, sc in each sc.
R. 13: Ch 1, decrease 1 sc at beginning and end of row. (To decrease, you skip one sc). [15 sc]
R. 14: Ch 1, work 15 sc.
R. 15: Ch 1, sc in 1st 5 sc.
R. 16 - 25: Ch 1, 5 sc. Cut yarn, pull end through loop.
Rejoin yarn @ sc # 6. Ch 1 and work 10 sc for 10 rows.
Now, work down opening:
Ch 4, skip 1 row, join ch with a slip stitch to next row.
Repeat from * - * 4 times. Cut yarn, pull end through the loop, and weave in ends.
Sew buttons or beads to front opening, matching them to the crocheted loops.

Back: Make 1
Ch 18.
R. 1: 1 sc in 2nd ch from hook, 1 sc in each ch. [17 sc]
R. 2 - 12: Ch 1, sc to end of row.
R. 13: Decrease 1 st at beginning and end of row. [15 sc]
R. 14 - 25: Ch 1, sc to end of row.
R. 26, 27, and 28 : Ch 1, sc in 3 sc. Cut yarn, pull end through loop, and weave in end.
Rejoin at other edge and repeat R. 26-28.

Sleeves: Make 2
Ch 16.
R. 1: Sc in 2nd ch from hook. Sc in each of next 14 ch [15 sc].
R. 2 - 21: Ch 1, sc in each sc in row.

Assembling Sweater
Sew front to back at shoulders. Center top edge of sleeve at shoulder center. Sew in place. Sew underarm seams and sweater's side seams.

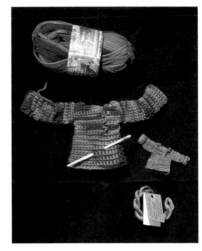

The Crocheted Sweater.

Wooden Knitting Needles

Did you know that you can make your own wooden knitting needles?

Dowels are available in quite small sizes at your hardware store (Lee Valley sells bundles of 6" long birch dowels that are 1/8" (approximately 3.75mm) and 1/12" (approximately 2.75mm) in diameter). Take a knitting gauge along to the hardware store to measure the dowels to make your favorite size knitting needles.

Cut the dowel to the length you prefer. Sharpen one end in a pencil sharpener. Sand the end to a less lethal point and sand the length of the needle, as well. Glue a bead (or other treasure) to the flat end and then oil or wax them. Voila! Magical, unique knitting needles. (I once had a dream that knitting needles were a magic wand, so I had to make some that had star beads on them.)

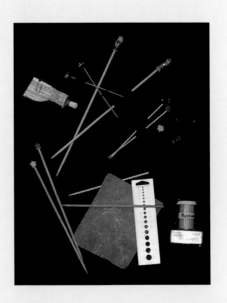

Madeleine Marian Jane, a Special Friend in the Garden

Whenever I do the guided visualization earlier in this chapter, the special friend I see in the garden is an interesting old woman. I have named her Madeleine Marian Jane, after three of my favorite authors. She is made exactly the same way as the Flat Soul Mate Doll (described on pages 11-14). I have drawn a face on the pattern, but feel free to draw a face of your own invention on this and all other doll patterns in the book. I knitted her sweater on 4mm needles, using Lily Sugar'n Cream #48, Mauve, following the basic pattern on page 15.

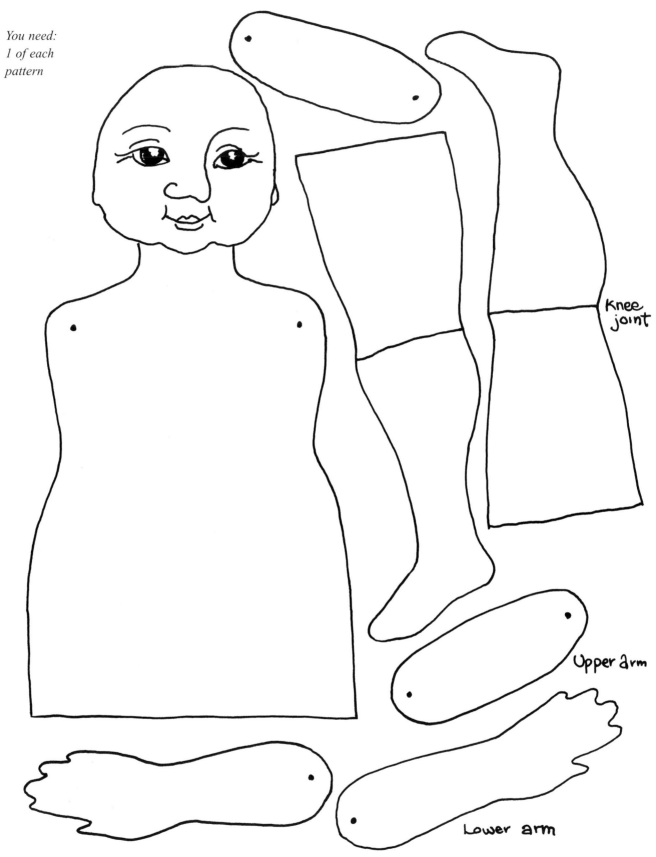

You need:
1 of each
pattern

knee joint

Upper arm

Lower arm

Madeleine Marion Jane Soul Mate Doll

Map Soul Mate Doll

At one point in my life, I went through a horrible upheaval. I felt like I was moving through a land that had no signposts or maps. It was a really grim time. A friend had an astute observation: "This is the fire that tempers your steel—think about how many times samurai swords go back into the flame and remember how beautiful they are in the end."

If you find yourself going the route of the samurai sword and moving into a new, uncharted direction, you may want to make yourself a Map Soul Mate Doll. She is a Basic Flat Soul Mate Doll, so use the templates on page 12, following the basic assembly instructions beginning on page 11.

When I was making my Map Soul Mate Doll, I was delighted by the curious names on the map. It's a 40-year-old map, showing the European exploration of Canada. Placing the body template so that the head was on Committee Bay seemed an extremely appropriate metaphor. This meant that Welcome Sound would be right at the doll's heart and the Bay of God's Mercy would be in her belly. I loved it. I couldn't resist giving her Meta Incognito or The Great Unknown for her right hand. Perhaps it would help her to "get a handle" on the Great Unknown.

The Map Soul Mate Doll can be a neat way of visualizing where you want to go in your life. Is there a place you would love to live or visit? Make a Map Soul Mate Doll with that place in her heart. Then, stop thinking of all of the things that are keeping you away from your dream destination. Focus on the "yes-ness" of that longed-for place and make that dream come true. Let your Map Soul Mate Doll lead you there—that's what maps are for.

Materials and Tools

Map
Glue
Scissors

1. Trace around the templates on the map.
2. Cut out the pieces and glue them to card stock if the map is on thin paper. Cut them out and glue the map to the other side of the pieces so that both sides have the map on them. Cut out. If the map is made of sturdy paper, you won't need to make it thicker with extra card stock.
3. Joint the shoulders. (See page 13 for instructions.) I chose to not have joints in the legs or at the elbows, but you can if you wish.

Serenity Soul Mate Doll

For those who enjoy sewing, the Flat Soul Mate Doll templates (see page 12) also work beautifully as a sewn doll. (The Soul Mate Angel Doll for Courage on page 77 also uses the Flat Soul Mate Doll templates, and is sewn, but in a totally different way.)

Serenity Soul Mate Dolls, wearing hand-woven dresses and a fabric dress.

I call the sewn and stuffed Soul Mate Doll made from the Flat Doll templates the Serenity Doll, because she was inspired by a very serene-looking old rag doll in a Celebration Room at a school I once visited. Because serenity struck me as being a good thing to aspire to, I came home and designed this doll. I can use all of the reminders of serenity I can get!

I love the quiet peacefulness of Amish dolls that have no facial features. There is a universal quality about the "open" face that one with individual features doesn't have. Of course, feel free to embroider or paint features on the face if you choose. Also, you can add any type of hair you wish.

Materials and Tools

Yarn*
Approximately 1/2 yd of
 muslin, linen, or other closely-
 woven fabric
Stuffing
Sewing machine or needle
 and thread
Pins
Scissors
Vanishing ink fabric marking
 pen
Paper clip
Small dowel or bamboo
 skewer

*Used in this project: *Kit Kin from the Caron Collection: Y.1 (white), Y.2 (black), Y.4 (Soft Brown); it takes two or three skeins of Kit Kin for each Soul Mate Doll or Bernat Handicrafter Crochet Cotton, #10, Ecru.*

1. Use a paper clip to temporarily join the upper and lower arm sections of the templates together so you can trace the arm as one piece.
2. Fold the fabric in half, right sides together. Leaving at least a 1/4" seam allowance around all of the pieces, trace around the body once, and twice around the leg and arm patterns, using the vanishing ink marker.

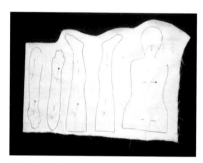

Tracing the templates onto fabric to make the Serenity Soul Mate Doll.

3. Sew along the outline of the body, leaving the bottom edge open for stuffing. Sew around the outline of the legs, leaving the top edge open for stuffing. Sew around the outline for the arms, leaving a 2" opening for stuffing along one side.
4. Cut out the body, arms, and legs, leaving a 1/4" seam allowance around each piece. Clip curved edges of the seam allowance. Turn right side out.
5. Lay the sewn leg on the leg pattern and draw a line across the knee with the vanishing ink marker.
6. To stuff the legs using the bamboo skewer or dowel, push tiny amounts of stuffing into them. Fill the legs to approximately 1" below the line. Stitch across the line. Finish by filling the legs with stuffing.

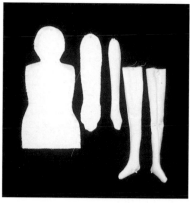

Making the knee joint.

7. Stuff the body. Fold a 1/4" edge up inside of the body's lower edge and pin the body together with one pin at the center of the body. Insert the top edge of the legs inside of the body's lower edge. Stitch in place across the front of the first leg. Stitch the body front to the body back at the center pin. Stitch across the front of the second leg and around and across the back of the legs.
8. Stuff arms and sew the opening shut. Stitch the inside top of the arm to the body at the shoulder. Optional: Draw finger lines on the hands and stitch through all layers to form fingers and thumbs.

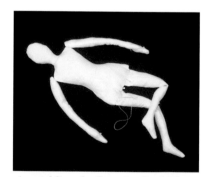

Assembling the Serenity Soul Mate Doll.

Note: The skirts, hanky dress, hat, and sweaters (pages 14-16) fit this doll.

Sewn Dress

Materials and Tools

Fabric
Optional: 12" of narrow lace
Optional: Approximately 1 yd
  vintage lace or ribbon
2 buttons, 1/4" in diameter
Sewing machine or needle
  and thread
Pins
Scissors
Vanishing ink fabric marking
  pen

1. Cut out a 12" by 18" piece of fabric for the skirt. Cut out a 6" by 8" rectangle of fabric for the bodice. Clean finish raw edges.

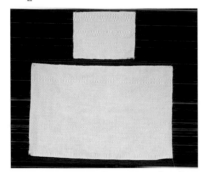

The bodice and skirt pieces for the sewn version of the dress for the Serenity Soul Mate Doll.

2. For the bodice, turn under a narrow hem along the 6" edges. Press and stitch. Sew lace to these edges. Fold the bodice section in half so that it is now

Sewn bodice with sleeves hemmed and neck hole cut and hemmed.

3" by 8". Cut a vertical slit down the front in the center. At the center horizontal line, which is the top of the sleeves, cut a 4" opening for the neck. This gives a T-shaped cut in the bodice. Hem these edges.

3. Make a pleat at the vertical center back of the bodice. Note that the pleat can be either on the inside or outside of the dress. Fold the bodice in half at the center back and sew 1" away from the fold. Flatten the fold and stitch the edges to the bodice back, centering the fold over the stitched line.

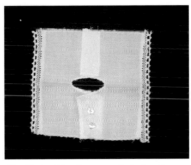

Bodice with pleat made in back.

4. Make two small buttonholes on the right-hand side of the bodice front. Overlap the right over the left by 1". Sew two small buttons to the left bodice front. Baste in place.

Underarms of sleeve sewn.

5. Turn bodice inside out. Sew sleeves by sewing from the sleeve edge to the "armpit" for 1".

6. For the fabric skirt, sew the center back seam along the 12" edge of the fabric. Hem the lower edge of the fabric or sew the narrow lace along it. Gather upper edge. With right sides together, sew skirt to bodice. You may wish to sew vintage lace or ribbon to the hem of the skirt.

Gather the skirt and sew to the bodice.

How to Make a Pin Board Loom

1. The backing board. You will need a board that is easy to push pins into, but strong enough that it will not bend or bow under the pressure of the warp. It also needs to be dense enough that the pins will stay in place as you weave. A couple of "macramé" boards, made from what appears to be compressed sawdust, I found in a second-hand store work well. I've also used dense pink and blue insulation foam boards that are an inch or two thick. Acoustical ceiling tiles work well, as long as you cover them with fabric, plastic wrap, or paper first to keep the dust down. In a pinch, taping three or four layers of sturdy corrugated cardboard together can work, but it's best to alternate the directions of the corrugations to increase the strength of the board.

2. Pins. Use sturdy straight pins or glass-headed pins, not T-pins (the "T" gets in the way).

3. Graph paper. Quarter-inch graph paper works fine for the projects in the book. Draw the outline of the finished piece and along the lower edge and mark a dot on each line of the graph paper. Along the upper edge, mark a dot at the center of each of the 1/4" squares. The pins will be inserted at these dots, at approximately a 30° angle, slanting away from the weaving. I number the dots, starting at the lower left-hand side. The first dot is #1. The first dot at the top is #2. The numbers at the bottom are always odd and the numbers at the top are always even.

*4. Warping the pin board loom. The warp is the yarn that goes lengthwise from pin to pin. You do your weaving on these threads. The weft is the yarn that goes across the warp, filling it in. It's a good idea to choose as smooth a yarn as possible for the warp. This way you won't make yourself crazy with splitting the warp as you are weaving. (Crochet cotton is great for the warp.) The weft can be the same as the warp, or it can be different colors or textures to create a pattern. You can also change the pattern of the weaving by changing the number of threads that you go over and under. **Always** start warping at pin #1. Tie the warp to the first pin, then follow the sequence of the numbered pins with the warp. Cut the warp and tie it to the last pin.*

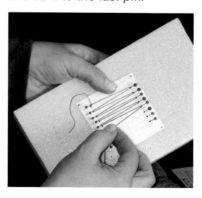

*5. Starting to weave.
a. Beginning at pin #1, thread a dull darning needle with a*

couple of feet of weft yarn. It's important to anchor the first and last rows of your weaving, so be sure that you go over/under across the row. Another way of working a foundation row is to do a row of Soumak weave, which is like the Blanket stitch in embroidery; bring the weft out over two warps and then go back around and behind one. Repeat across the row.

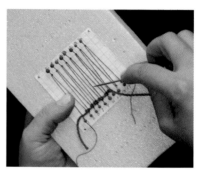

*b. When you have worked across the row, you will begin by weaving over and under the warp, back and forth. Don't pull the weft tight across the weaving, because this will pull in the edges; angle the weft up slightly as you go across, leaving an arch of weft. This allows the weft to settle in around the warp. You can either weave in the ends of the weft as you go, or you may prefer to weave the ends into the weft channels of the weaving when it's complete. A small latch hook is handy to pull the ends in.
c. To speed up weaving, I use two little 6" steel rulers I bought at a hardware store as shed sticks. You weave them into the warp, and when you turn them on their side, they open a shed (the space where the weft goes) for you to zoom your needle or shuttle through. I weave the first ruler in over*

and under, and push it to the top of the weaving. This one stays in the weaving as long as possible. The second ruler is for the second shed, and is woven into every other row, used to open the shed, and then pulled out. It can't stay in, because it would interfere with the first shed.

d. When weaving a piece that has the warp tied on in several sections, such as the Mermaid's tail on page 109, I always tie the weft to the warp when I weave up to a new warp end.

e. Beating: Push the weft into place at the lower edge of the weaving, with the point of your darning needle or a table fork. Start beating (tapping) at the side you entered on the row, working toward your shuttle or needle.

f. When you have filled the warp with the weft, be sure to "capture" the warp ends so they won't slip down into a channel of weft. You do this by weaving over one, then under one, warp strand. Working a row of Soumak across the top of the weaving and tying a knot to the single warp at the side works well. Remove the pins. Very lightly steam with a pressing cloth between the weaving and the iron.

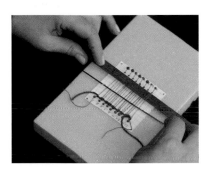

Joining Pieces With the Baseball Stitch

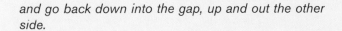

This is a good choice for joining edges. Hold the two pieces with their wrong sides together. Starting at the right-hand side, make a V-shaped stitch. Bring the needle up from the gap to the outside of one side...

and go back down into the gap, up and out the other side.

Woven Dress

Materials and Tools

2 balls of worsted weight "dishcloth" yarn (approx 2 oz. each)*
2 buttons, 1/4" in diameter
Approximately 1 yd of vintage lace
Lap Loom A, pin board loom**, or Weavette Loom
Darning needle
Needle and thread
Pins
Narrow ruler or small knitting needle

*Used in this project: *The blue dress was woven with Lily Sugar'n Cream #170 Winterberry and #181 Faded Denim. The cream-colored dress was woven with Lily Sugar'n Cream #180 Peppercorn and #14 Ecru*

***For the pin board loom, you will need a piece of sturdy pink or blue foam insulation board, at least 1" thick, or a ceiling tile that's been wrapped with plastic wrap and taped to lessen the dust coming off it. The board should be about 14" long by 7" wide. You will also need a piece of 14" long by 7" wide 1/4" graph paper. Pin this paper to the board. Insert pins for 4-1/2" along a line 1" from the lower edge of the paper. Insert pins for 4-1/2", 12" from the lower edge. This is the pin board loom for the skirt sections. You'll rearrange the pins to weave the bodice sections.*

1. For the skirt, if you are using the Lap Loom, weave two 9" by 12" pieces. The edges are pre-finished. If you are using a pin board loom, weave four 12" by 4-1/2" pieces. Sew the four panels together to form a skirt that is 12" from the hem to the bodice edge and 18" around. If you would like to use a Weavette Loom, use the 4" by 6" rectangular loom and weave nine rectangles. Sew them together to make the 12" by 18" panel for the skirt.

The parts of the hand-woven dress (including vintage handmade lace for the hem).

2. Make the woven bodice using either the Lap Loom or pin board loom (see page 24 for directions). Weave three pieces, one piece 3" by 6" and two 3" by 4". If you are using a Weavette Loom, the bodice pieces will be slightly larger because of the loom's size. You will weave a 4" by 6" rectangle for the back of the bodice and two 4" squares for the front. Assemble these pieces in the same way as the smaller ones.

a. Start by tying on a 6" wide warp. Weave 3" for the bodice/sleeve back section. Slip the warp off two pegs at both sides of the top of the loom. Tie a square knot in these "freed" warps at the upper edge of the woven piece. This leaves a 4" wide warp for the front pieces. Cut a strip of card stock 3" by 8" or 9". This is a spacer. Open a shed, slip the spacer into the warp, and weave 3" for the first bodice/front section.

b. Make another spacer and insert it into the warp. Turn the loom around so that the top is now at the bottom (so you don't have so far to reach while weaving). With a darning needle, weave the last 3" section for the other bodice/front section.

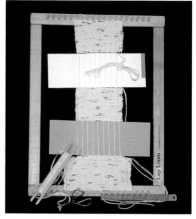

The bodice parts being woven on the Lap Loom.

c. Lift the weaving off the loom. Pull out the spacers and cut the warp in the center of the spaces. Tie square knots across the ends of the warps. With a darning needle, thread the warp ends down through the weft channels.

d. The 3" by 6" piece is the back of the sleeves and bodice. Lay the two 3" by 4" pieces on top of the bodice back, overlapping the right over the left. Sew buttons to the left side. Make buttonholes on the right. Sew the upper edge, leaving 1" open at the center for the neck. Sew the lower edge of the sleeve for 1" from the outside edge to the armpit, leaving 4" open at the center. Gather the upper edge of the skirt and sew to the bodice. Sew the vintage lace to the hem.

Pah Shaw Soul Mate Doll

This is my version of the Pah Shaw Doll. She is also made with the Flat Doll technique, exactly the same way as the Basic Flat Doll (page 11) with one exception: in order to get that all-important flip of the wrist, one of the hands is jointed at the wrist. The wrist joint is made just like the hip and knee joints, with a small strip of fabric that needs to be painted. Before embellishing her, as described on the following page, paint or color her face and feet.

Materials and Tools

Card stock
Vintage lace or other fabric
Vintage ribbons
Seed beads
Small scraps of white fabric
Short lengths of lightweight
  brass or copper wire
Chenille stem
Paint or colored ink
Paper
Charms*, buttons, etc.
Star stickers
Needlenose pliers
Scissors
Wire snips
Craft knife
Cutting mat
Ruler
Paper clips (plastic-covered
  that match blouse)
Hot glue gun and sticks
Glue
Needle and thread
Paint brushes
Colored pencils
Awl

*Used in this project: *"Mini Star" charms from Birdhouse Enterprises.*

Pah Shaw's wrist joint before painting.

1. Hair: Use strands of 100 seed beads. Gather them up and hold them in place with short lengths of chenille stem. Glue them in place before gluing the hat on.

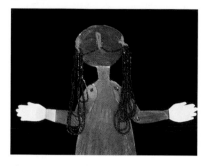

Arranging and gluing on the bead strands for Pah Shaw's hair.

2. Earrings: Pierce the dots in her ears and insert short lengths of wire. Bend the wires into a hoop with needlenose pliers.

3. Hat: Gather vintage embroidered ribbon or strips of fabric. Glue a narrow ribbon over the gathered edge.

Gather ribbons for Pah Shaw's hat.

4. Skirt: Gather vintage lace with a narrow ribbon and glue in place. Glue a wide ribbon over the waist.

Pah Shaw's skirt is gathered onto a narrow ribbon, and wide ribbon is glued over the waist.

5. Blouse: Paint on her blouse. Glue charms and star stickers to it. Refer to the photos for placing her blouse trim, like additional embroidered ribbon.

6. To hang her on the wall, take a piece of wire (approximately 9" long) and bend it in half with needlenose pliers. This is the hanging loop. Fold a hook at each end, then spread the wires enough to fit under her arms, adjusting them to fit and support her. Squeeze the hooks firmly to hold her body without wiggling. The hanging loop may need to be bent out slightly. You can also hang other Soul Mate Dolls in this manner.

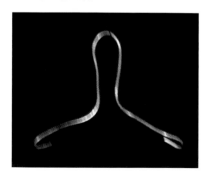

Bend a wire to make a doll hanger.

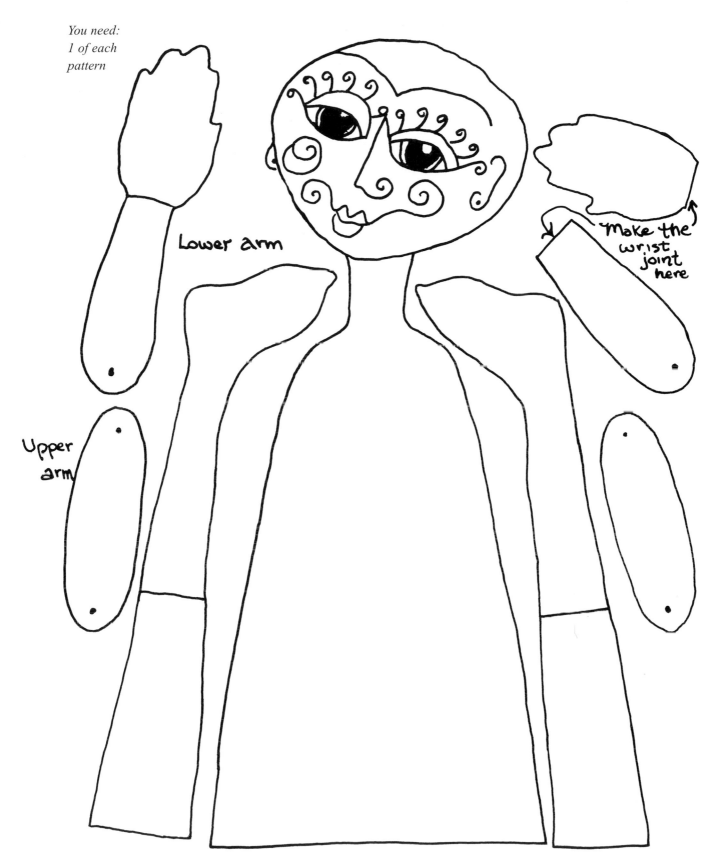

You need:
1 of each
pattern

Lower arm

Upper arm

Make the wrist joint here

Pah Shaw Soul Mate Doll

2 chapter

The Power of Story

Soul Mate Dollmaking is all about becoming more creative. One way to enter the realm of creativity is to find a story with imagery that appeals to you and then to explore that story and those images. But, before we begin with story, there is something I want to talk to you about: the gateway to creativity and the gatekeeper. These are very powerful metaphors, and we will be making a Gatekeeper Soul Mate Doll to remember the importance of opening and closing.

In my own life, I've learned about the gatekeeper from our own gate. We live in the country and have dogs and horses, so a closed gate at the end of our driveway is very important. Yet, it is a little tiresome to have to stop the car, get out, open the gate, move the car, get out, and close the gate before being able to leave.

One of the small rituals of kindness that has evolved in our family is the "I'll get the gate for you" one. This requires you to, first of all, notice that the other person is preparing for takeoff, then to stop whatever you're doing. Then, there is the changing of footwear and grabbing of a coat before the trundle down the driveway.

This small changing of gears actually is a large gift to both the driver and the gatekeeper. The driver feels blessed by the gift of time and loving kindness of the gatekeeper. The gatekeeper feels a sense of tenderness to be seeing the loved one leaving, for however brief or long a time. Then, there is the bonus of the sudden silence, and depending on the time of day and the season, the gifts of being in nature, like the rustling of leaves, the songs of birds or frogs, or the shimmering of stars.

How does this relate to the quest for creativity in one's life? Well, there is definitely a gate at the threshold to the world of imagination and creativity. It, too, requires a gatekeeper. As that gatekeeper, what do you have to *stop* doing in order to open the gate for yourself? There may be a million reasons, a million excuses why you are too busy to go there. Believe me, it is worth it to take the time, change gears, and stroll down to the gate. Opening the gate also requires you to close it as well, to keep the "dogs and horses" of the everyday world from ambushing you. Take the time—it's worth it!

The Gatekeeper Soul Mate Doll

The Gatekeeper Soul Mate Doll wears a hat crocheted in embroidery floss with a 3.75mm crochet hook, using the Basic Crocheted Hat pattern on page 15. She wears an embroidered vest, and because the only kind of embroidery that I do nowadays is punch-style with the Igolochkoy needle, that's what you'll see in the photo. Feel free to make her hat and vest in any style or technique that appeals to you.

To make the Gatekeeper Soul Mate Doll, refer to the Basic Soul Mate Doll on page 11. I chose to not make knee joints for her and painted on the boots.

Materials and Tools

Card stock
Brown paper (or your choice of decorative paper)
2 spools each of black, rose, and teal thread
Closely-woven cotton fabric
Heart and key charms*
Craft glue
Colored pencils
3.75mm crochet hook
1 skein embroidery floss
Igolochkoy embroidery needle, "one-strand" size
2 paper clips
Hot glue gun and glue sticks
Scissors
Permanent black fine-point marker

*Used in this project: *"Victorian I" brass charms from Birdhouse Enterprises.*

Vest

1. Trace the pattern onto closely-woven cotton fabric. Feel free to change the pattern in any way. I worked it in punch needle-style embroidery, using an Igolochkoy "one-strand" embroidery needle. I used two strands of sewing machine thread, changing shades to give depth to the embroidery. I also nipped the tiniest bit of the depth gauge off my needle (the black plastic tube on the needle) to make the pile a little deeper.

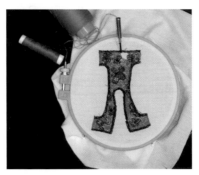

Embroidering the Gatekeeper's vest.

2. After the vest is embroidered, cut it out, leaving a 1/4" seam allowance all around it. Clip curved edges. Turn in the seam allowances around the front and neck edges, arm holes, and lower edges. Using fairly small stitches, hand-stitch them to the wrong side of the vest. Sew the side seams together. Glue the vest to the doll. Put the heart charm on a piece of thread and tie it around her neck and glue the key charm to her hand.

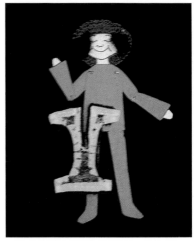

Seam allowances are cut around the edges of the vest and then are turned and stitched in place.

Stories are tools and they are medicine. They have the power to hurt or heal us. Think about when someone tells you a disturbing story—it leaves you feeling diminished. But, a story full of heart and soul can soothe and inspire.

There are stories that can help us reinvent our personal mythology and restore our personal sense of delight and feelings of "yes-ness." They can be the stories of historical, mythical, or even fictional heroines. The stories of their journeys can help us map out our own journey.

I believe that we need the stories and images of wonderful heroines in our lives. They truly are our soul mates! One such story of a very special soul mate happens to be one of my personal favorites, and I am going to tell you my version of it now.

You need:
1 of each
pattern

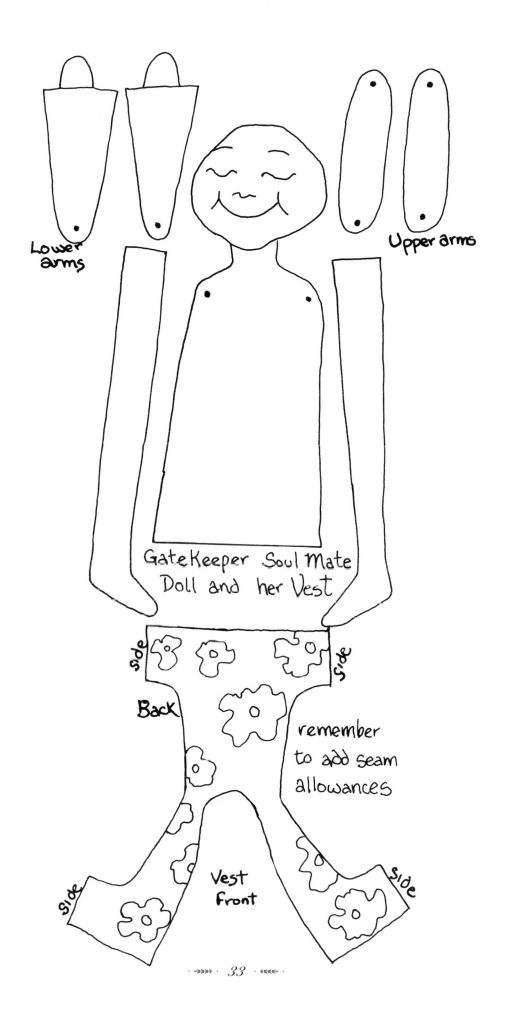

Lower arms

Upper arms

GateKeeper Soul Mate
Doll and her Vest

side

side

Back

remember
to add seam
allowances

side

Vest
Front

side

Once and twice and possibly not so long ago, Molly Whuppie and her two older sisters went into the woods because their parents could not care for them. They became lost and ended up at the house of a wicked giant.

After supper he placed three gold chains around the necks of his daughters. He twisted three straws around the necks of Molly Whuppie and her sisters.

When everyone was asleep, Mollie Whuppie slipped the gold chains off the necks of the sleeping giant girls and put them around her sisters' necks and her own. Then she took the straw chains and put them around the necks of the Giant's daughters. The evil Giant, feeling the straw chains, tied up all his own girls in a sack and made off with them.

Mollie Whuppie and her sisters threw off the gold chains and ran and ran until they came to a deep chasm they could not cross, for there was no bridge.

Mollie Whuppie pulled one hair from her head, picked up a stick, and using it as a spindle, started to spin the hair with it. The hair got longer and longer and stronger and stronger. Then she cast the one hair across the great divide and made the One Hair Bridge. They ran across it and they ran and ran until they came to a castle.

Mollie Whuppie told the King her story. The King said to Mollie Whuppie, "Mollie Whuppie, I have a problem. You are a clever girl. You have done

well, and that's a fine thing. But, there is a better thing, and that's to steal the sword that hangs above the Giant's bed."

"I agree, sir, that would be a fine thing, and easily done."

The King was pleased. "In exchange for this brave deed, I'll give the hand of my oldest son to your oldest sister in marriage."

Mollie Whuppie asked the two, "Does this suit you?" It did indeed. So, into the woods she went. Soon she was at the house of the sleeping Giant. She climbed up the headboard and took the sword in her hands. She stumbled, and the Giant jumped up. Mollie Whuppie ran and the Giant ran and they both ran and ran right to the One Hair Bridge, and Mollie Whuppie ran across it, but the Giant could not. He shouted, "Woe betide ye, Mollie Whuppie, if ye ever come back again!"

Mollie Whuppie called, "I come and I go, whenever needs must, and that is so!"

She carried the sword to the King and the King's oldest son married Mollie Whuppie's oldest sister. Then, the King said to Mollie Whuppie, "Ah, Mollie Whuppie, that was a fine thing and done well. But, there's another thing that needs doing, and that would even be better. Steal the purse that lies under the Giant's pillow. And, as my second son seems to be smitten with your second sister, I would give him in marriage to her."

This suited them well, so back she went to the Giant's house. She slid her hand under the Giant's pillow and locked her fingers around the strings of the purse. She ran for the door, and the Giant jumped up and ran, and they both ran and ran until they came to the One Hair Bridge and Mollie Whuppie ran across it, but the Giant could not.

He stood on one side and stomped and cursed at Mollie Whuppie, "Woe betide ye, Mollie Whuppie, if ye ever come here again."

"I come and I go, whenever needs must, and that is so!"

Mollie Whuppie took the purse back to the King, who was very pleased, and so were all of the people whose money the Giant had stolen.

Then, the middle prince married Mollie Whuppie's middle sister.

The King said, "Mollie Whuppie, that was a fine thing you did, and you did it well. But I know of a finer, but harder thing. Steal the ring the dreadful Giant wears upon his finger. That would be a splendid thing, Mollie Whuppie. And if you do it, I would give you the hand of my youngest son in marriage."

This suited Mollie Whuppie and the youngest prince so she agreed to it. Off she went to the Giant's house. She ran a sliver of soap round the Giant's finger, and the ring slipped off. The Giant woke with a roar and shook her hard.

"Aha! Mollie Whuppie! Once too many is never again!" he shouted at her. "If I'd done the ills to you as you have done to me, what would you be doing to me?"

Mollie Whuppie's brains rattled inside her head and she remembered his daughters all tied up in a sack. He shook her again, and the words fell out of her,

"I guess you're going to tie me up in a sack, too!"

"Ay, that I am, Mollie Whuppie, and I'm going to give you a boating, too, for all my troubles." He threw her in a sack, and the dog and the cat and a pair of scissors, too, for in his anger he was snatching up anything in his reach.

"Ugh," thought Mollie Whuppie, and she squeezed her eyes tight. Stars danced inside her eyelids. "Now, that's odd," she thought. "Many's a time I've squeezed my eyes, but I've never seen the stars dance so. It must be this sack that does it."

She was so interested in the stars, that she cried out, "Oh, what I see, it looks so fine!"

The Giant's wife sat up in surprise. "What's that you say, Mollie Whuppie?"

"Oh, what I see, it looks so fine!"

"Now, Mollie Whuppie, you can't see anything, for it's as dark as pitch inside that sack!"

"But I see the stars all dancing so!"

"Let me see, Mollie Whuppie!"

So, Mollie Whuppie grabbed the scissors and cut open the sack. She hopped out of the sack, the dog and the cat jumped out, and the Giantess clambered in. She pulled the sack tight about herself. "Why, Mollie Whuppie, you're right, I do see the stars when I'm in here!"

The Giant stomped into the house with a huge cudgel. Mollie Whuppie ran and hid. The Giant roared at the sack, "Take that, Mollie Whuppie!" and thumped the sack with the cudgel.

The Giantess shot out of the sack, punching and screaming, "It's me you fool!"

Mollie Whuppie decided it was time to leave and ran out the door. The Giant saw her and ran, and they both ran and ran to the One Hair Bridge. Mollie Whuppie ran across, but the Giant could not. He heaved a great boulder up over his head and bellowed at Mollie Whuppie, "Great the harms you've done me, Mollie Whuppie! And if you were me, then what would you do to quench this rage?"

"Well, I'd gobble that huge boulder and then I'd drink the river dry!"

So, the Giant gobbled up the

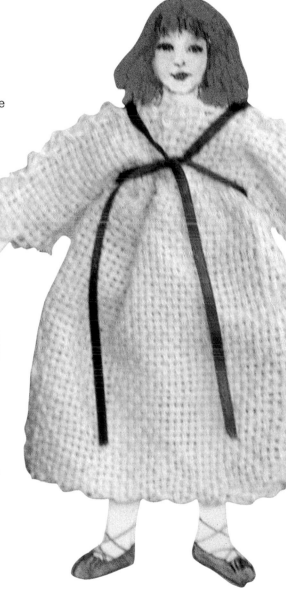

boulder and put his head down in the river and slurped until the river ran dry. When he tried to get up again, he found he could not, so he lie there, kicking and cursing until he burst. And so he never troubled anyone again.

Mollie Whuppie carried the ring home to the King. She and her handsome young prince danced with joy at their wedding. Folk from miles around came to celebrate with them. And so it was that Mollie Whuppie and her prince, and all of the people of the kingdom, lived long and well, and that's the story of Molly Whuppie for you.

———————

I love this story and return to it often. It's an enigma and there is much below the surface. We understand without being told that the three objects Mollie Whuppie must steal are power objects. We assume that the Giant should not be in posses-

sion of them and that somehow things are out of balance because he has them. Otherwise, Mollie Whuppie would be the villain and he the poor set-upon victim.

Mollie Whuppie is a trickster. She is a wonderfully illogical character—a positive heroine who blithely accepts that in order to set things right, she must become a thief. She is the youngest of three abandoned, homeless sisters, and is also the bravest.

Her greatest achievement, I believe, is not that she is able to steal the wicked Giant's power objects, but that she is able to cross the great divide. She shows us how to make a leap of faith, how to spin a One Hair Bridge, when necessary. So, this is a story about making connections and building bonds.

Personally, if the King had asked me to go back to the evil Giant's house, again and again and again, I would have invited him to hold his nose and leap into the great divide. Mollie Whuppie understands that the King (and his army) cannot cross the great divide. The army and the Giant would probably lay waste the

entire kingdom in bashing one another to bits. But notice one important thing: the King doesn't order Mollie Whuppie to complete the three tasks. He *asks* her if she is willing to restore balance by stealing the power objects.

Mollie Whuppie is a remarkably efficient agent of restoration. She is a perfect example of feistiness. She actively lives her life, trusting her instincts and using her wits. She chooses her life and lives it with gusto. She quickly learns to navigate, in the darkness, a strange land. She creates a home for herself and commits herself to love. What a great role model!

———————

And wouldn't it be wonderful to be able to see Mollie Whuppie every day and hold her in our hands? That's why we're going to make a Mollie Whuppie Soul Mate Doll. Refer to the instructions on page 11 for the Basic Flat Soul Mate Doll. If you wish to crochet her a hat, you'll find the instructions on page 15, and see page 137 for instructions to make her basket. After you've made yourself a Mollie Whuppie Soul Mate Doll, think of a few other heroines and make Soul Mate Dolls of them, too!

Mollie Whuppie Soul Mate Doll

Materials and Tools

Card stock (because she is so small, fairly lightweight card stock works fine)
White paper
Paper clips or 18-gauge wire
Sharp craft knife
Cutting mat
Awl
Scissors
Glue
Needlenose pliers
Paint and brushes, colored pencils, or crayons

1. Copy the pattern and glue it to the card stock.

2. Glue plain white paper to the other side. Allow the glue to dry completely.

3. Cut out the doll.

4. Make the leg joints (refer to the Basic Flat Doll instructions, page 13).

5. Color or paint the front of the doll parts, turn them over, and color the backs, matching the neckline of the chemise, hair, and shoulder joints.

6. Refer to Basic Flat Doll instructions (page 13) to make shoulder joints.

Dress

I wove her dress on the Lacis Square Loom. I wanted a fine weave to be in scale with her small size, so I used a grid of eight squares to the inch to set up the pins in the loom, rather than the six squares to the inch that the loom comes with. You could also weave the dress on a pin board loom (see page 24). If you choose to weave it on the pin board loom, set your pins at 1/8" intervals, rather than 1/4". If you don't want to weave her dress, use these dimensions to develop your own pattern to sew from fabric: for the skirt, weave two 4" squares, and for the bodice and sleeves, weave four 1-1/8" by 2-3/4" rectangles.

Materials and Tools

Embroidery floss or light-weight cotton yarn*
16" narrow ribbon, braid, or yarn
Lacis Square Loom or pin board loom
Scissors

*Used in this project: *Small amount of Bernat Handicrafter Crochet Cotton #10, Ecru; 2 skeins of Caron Wildflowers #72.*

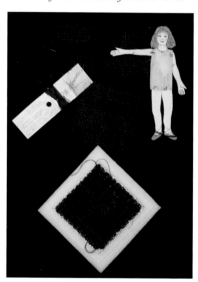

Mollie Whuppie with the Lacis Square Loom and the parts of her dress.

1. Sew the short edge of the two sleeve pieces together for the center back of the bodice and sleeves.

2. Pull up the last row of the weaving to gather the upper edge of the skirt back so that it is 2-1/2". Pin the center top of the skirt to the center of the bodice back. The sleeves will stick out on either side of skirt.

3. Lay the front bodice/sleeve pieces on top of the back pieces. Sew the upper edges of the sleeves together, leaving 1" open at the center for the neck.

4. Pull up the last row of the weaving to gather the upper edge of the skirt front so it is also 2-1/2". Pin the center of the skirt's top to the center of the bodice front. Sew the sleeve/bodice fronts to the skirt front.

5. Sew skirt sides together. Sew remaining sleeve edges.

Mollie Whuppie's dress sewn together.

6. Put the dress on the doll. Wrap the 16" length of narrow ribbon, braid, or yarn around her waist and tie it at center back. Bring the ends over her shoulders. Slip one end under the center of the ribbon at the waist front. Tie a knot.

Tying the ribbon around Mollie Whuppie's dress.

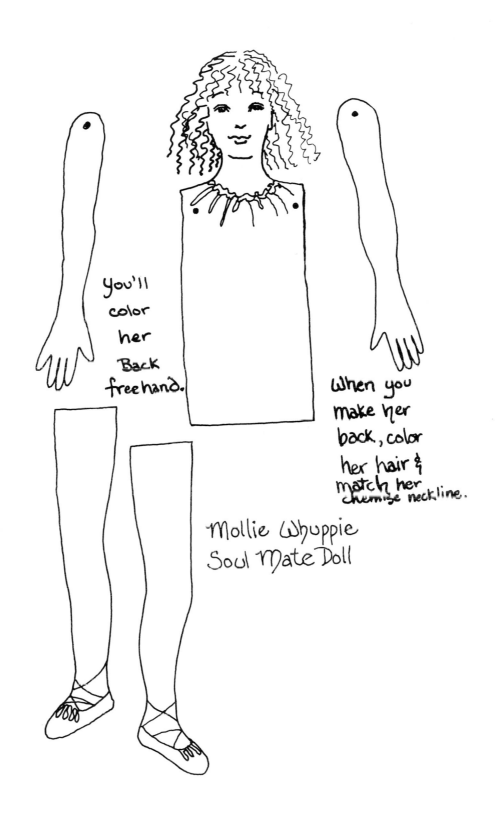

You'll color her Back freehand.

When you make her back, color her hair & match her chemise neckline.

Mollie Whuppie Soul Mate Doll

Pocket Soul Mate Dolls

There is another heroine story that I particularly like. It's a Russian folktale, about a Cinderella-type character called Vasilisa. I am so fond of the story because Vasilisa is guided and assisted through tremendous difficulties by a wise little doll that her dying mother made for her. Vasilisa carries it in her pocket and it comforts, teaches, and counsels her, ultimately guiding her to great happiness.

I have long been a fan of pocket dollies. In fact, when I make myself a new garment, I always include at least one pocket that's large enough for a doll. I hope these will bring you pleasure. Because they are so small, they are very portable and quick to make.

Make her uniquely your own by changing anything about her. Try your hand at drawing your own version of her face. Feel free to make her larger or smaller. Change her proportions if you like. In this project, I embroidered these dolls with the Igolochkoy embroidery needle, which is a hollow, hand-made brass needle. It gives them the loveliest dense pile, rather like terry toweling. The metallic "Antica" threads I used make it look a little like beading. It's important to use a closely-woven (never knit) fabric and to pull it tight as a drum in your embroidery hoop.

I worked the orange-haired dolls with three strands of Bernat embroidery floss, using the three-strand needle. I cut approximately 1-yard lengths of floss and divided them in half to make the three-strand lengths. The dark-haired Pocket Soul Mate Dolls were embroidered with Wildflowers Royal Jewels, Passion, Winter Wheat, and Antica AT4 and AT5 from the Caron Collection, using the one-strand Igolochkoy needle.

Embroidered Pocket Soul Mate Doll

Materials and Tools

6" by 7" piece of cotton or other closely-woven fabric in the skin tone of your choice
1 skein embroidery floss
Beads, buttons, shells, charms, etc.
Igolochkoy needle
Scissors
Embroidery hoop
Needle and thread
Pins
Stuffing
Small dowel or bamboo skewer
Fine-point permanent black marker

1. Trace the pattern onto the fabric with the permanent marker. Draw the body on the wrong side of the fabric. Flip the fabric over to the right side to draw the face. When drawing the face, touch the fabric lightly with the marker to minimize ink "bleeding." To make the back, omit the face when tracing the pattern. Be sure to leave at least a 1/4" seam allowance around each piece.

2. Stretch the fabric tightly in the embroidery hoop, wrong side up, because the Igolochkoy is worked from the back. Feel free to use your favorite embroidery method. Embroider the front and back.

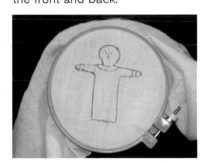

Preparing to embroider a Pocket Doll.

3. To make her hair, slip the red tube off the needle. Work one row of hair around the sides and top of face. Fill in the back of the head with hair.

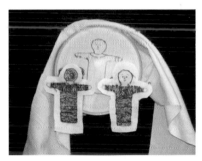

An embroidered Pocket Doll, with seam allowances cut.

4. Cut out the front and back, leaving a 1/4" seam allowance around each piece. Clip at the neck and underarms. Fold seam allowances in and pin them to make it easier to sew the hands.
5. Pin the doll front to the back, right sides out, and hand-sew together with the Baseball stitch (page 25), leaving the lower edge open for stuffing.
6. Stuff very lightly, using the dowel or skewer to insert the stuffing. Sew the lower edge closed.

A faster variation of the Pocket Soul Mate Doll is to paint, instead of embroider, it.

Materials and Tools

6" by 7" piece of closely-woven cotton fabric (I usually don't paint the dolls' faces, so I choose a color that is a skin tone I like for that particular doll.)
Optional: ribbon or lace
Embroidery floss
Embroidery hoop
Scissors
Needle
Acrylic or fabric paints (you can even use nail polish!) and paint brushes
Fine-point permanent black felt-tip marker
Stuffing

1. Trace the pattern on paper and make a template by gluing it to card stock or plastic. (Lids from food containers work well for the template.) Pin two layers of fabric together, with the right sides together. Trace around the template with a vanishing ink marker and sew on the outline by hand or machine, leaving an opening for stuffing.

Tracing the painted Pocket Doll.

2. Trim away the excess fabric, leaving a 1/4" seam allowance. Clip under arms and at the neck. Turn right side out. Stuff. Draw on the face with the permanent black felt-tip marker.

Sewing the painted Pocket Doll.

3. Paint the body and embroider on hair. The hair is worked with embroidery floss around the face on the right side of the face. Hold a knitting needle or dowel up against the head and stitch loops around it. This gives uniformity to the loop length. The back of the head can either be painted or covered with straight stitches. Trim dress with ribbon or lace if desired.

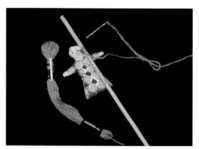

Stitching around a dowel to make the hair for the painted Pocket Doll.

You need:
Embroidered: 1 pattern, for front and back
Painted: 1 pattern on doubled fabric

Pocket Soul Mate Dolls

Pouches for Pocket Dolls

What if you don't have a pocket for your pocket doll? Make a pouch to pop her into!

The Pouch With Black Cord and Beads

The pouch will be 3" square, with a 2" flap. It was woven on a Lap Loom, but you could set up a pin board loom with a 3" wide by 8" long warp for this pouch.

Materials and Tools

Black cotton yarn* (worsted weight "dishcloth" yarn; approx. 2 oz.)
1 skein contrasting cotton yarn or embroidery floss**
Seed beads
Lap Loom or pin board loom***
Sewing machine thread
Darning needle
Ruler
Scissors
Optional: crochet hook or small latch hook
Fork (this works well to tap the weft into place)
Embroidery needle
Optional: shuttle
Optional: metal rulers or metal knitting needle
Small clamp

*Used in this project: *Lily Sugar'n Cream #2 Black; **Caron's Watercolours Royal Jewel.*

****For the pin board loom, you will need a piece of high-density foam or insulation board that is 5" by 10". You will also need a 5" by 10" piece of 1/4" graph paper and twenty-six pins. Place this paper on the board. One inch from the side and 1" from the lower edge, insert thirteen pins, one every 1/4". One inch from the side and 1" from the top edge, insert one pin (total thirteen pins)*

every 1/4" for 3". This gives a weaving area of 3" by 8".

1. On your loom, with the black thread, make a 3" wide warp.
First row: Work a row of Soumak weave in black.
Weave 1" in black and 2" in contrasting color.
Work a row of Soumak weave in black.
Weave 3" more in black.
Work a row of Soumak weave in black.
Weave 2" in contrasting color.
(The weaving now measures 3" by 8".)

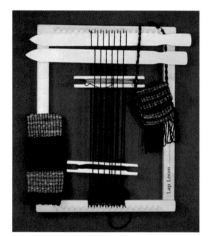

Weaving a pouch for the Pocket Dolls on a Lap Loom.

2. Remove from the loom. Tie square knots in the warp ends across the end of the weaving. With a small crochet hook, latch hook, or darning needle, weave the warp ends into the weft channels.
3. Fold the pouch at the second Soumak weaving line. Stitch the sides together. Make a twisted cord by twisting together three strands of 72" long black cotton (see the following page). Fold in half, allow it to twist around itself, and tie a knot in the loose ends. Sew the cord along the pouch's side edges.

4. The beaded fringe is made by stringing eighty seed beads per loop and stitching the loop to the Soumak weaving line at the bottom fold.

The Silver Pouch

This was woven on the Lacis Square Loom, set up to weave 3" squares. You also could set up a pin board loom with 3" squares or use a square Weavette Loom.

Materials and Tools

2-3 skeins of silver embroidery floss*
1 skein of metallic embroidery floss**
Approximately 25-30 grams of seed beads
Optional: vintage button
Lacis Square Loom, pin board loom***, or Weavette Loom (2" or 4" square)****
Scissors
Darning needle
Ruler
Small clamp
Beading needle

Used in this project: I used two skeins of Pewter Watercolours by Caron, but this was tight, so you might want to use an extra skein. I also used one skein of Antica, AT3 from Caron**.*

****For a pin board loom, set it up 3" wide by 3" high. You will need a piece of dense foam or insulation board that's about 5" square. You will also need a 5" square piece of 1/4" graph paper and twenty-six pins. Place the paper on the board. Place pins every 1/4" for 3". Then 3" above the first line of pins, place another row of*

pins every 1/4" for 3".
****If you are weaving this
pouch on a Weavette Loom, you
will use the 2" square to make a
tiny pouch or the 4" square loom
to make a slightly larger one.
Assembly is the same as for the 3"
squares.*

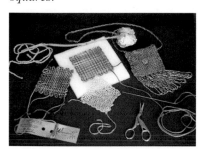

*Weaving a pouch for the Pocket
Dolls on the Lacis Square Loom.*

1. Weave two squares with
silver embroidery floss and one

with the metallic embroidery
floss. Sew three edges of the
two silver squares together to
make the body of the pouch.
2. Bead the lower edge. I used
silver seed beads that I cut off
of Auntie Donna's old pink polyester dress. Each loop of beads
is 100 beads long. To speed
things up, I measured 100
beads and found this to be
about 6" long. I quit counting
and just measured them as I
threaded and stitched them to
the pouch.
3. The cord was made with
three strands of metallic floss
that were about 70" long,
twisted, folded, and knotted.
Then the cord was sewn to the
sides of the pouch. Bury the

knot inside the pouch.
Pull the metallic square into a
diamond shape and sew half of
it to the back of the pouch. Fold
the remaining triangle-shaped
half over the front. If you have a
favorite vintage button, you
might choose to use it to close
the pouch.

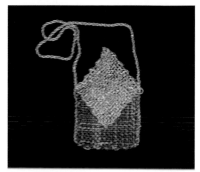

*Sewing the "flap" square onto the
silver pouch.*

How to Make a Twisted Cord

1. Cut three or four lengths of yarn, each approximately 72" long.
2. Clamp one end of the strands to a solid surface.
3. Twist the other end of the strands until you can't twist anymore.
4. Hold your finger at the center of the strands and loop them over your finger so you keep tension
on the twisted strands while you are folding the "twisted ends" toward the clamped ends.
5. Hold the twisted ends at the clamp with one hand while the folded end starts to spin around
itself, forming a twisted cord.
6. When the cord has stopped spinning, release the clamped ends and tie a knot to fasten the ends
together securely.

Rabbit, Cat, and Flower
Soul Mate Doll Chairs

When I think of good stories, like Mollie Whuppie's, I think of curling up in a wonderful chair to read or better yet, to listen to it. So, I designed three chairs for Soul Mate Dolls to sit in. I wanted to make magical chairs that anyone could make without carpentry tools (or skills). I sat and doodled in my sketchbook until these three chairs emerged. If you have the tools and inclination to make these chairs in wood, you can adapt the instructions for the woodworking shop.

Minnaloushe naps among the Soul Mate Doll Chairs.

Materials and Tools for the Chair Sides

11" by 17" piece of corrugated cardboard for each chair
Card stock
Paints, crayons, or colored pencils
4-1/2" long (1/8" diameter) dowels, 3 for each chair (or 3 bamboo skewers cut to 4-1/2" long)
Vanishing marker
Tape
Awl
Sharp craft knife
Cutting mat
Scissors
Hole punch
Paint brushes
Hot glue gun and sticks

1. Copy patterns. Join the two parts of each chair pattern at the dotted lines with tape to make the complete pattern. Glue pattern to card stock to make a template. Cut out.

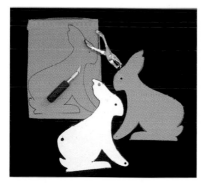

The pattern for the Rabbit Chair is joined together and a template made. One side is traced and the other is cut out. Use a hole punch to punch the eye hole and an awl to pierce holes for the dowels.

2. Trace the template onto sturdy card stock, flip it over, and trace a reverse of it.
3. Cut out both sides from cardboard. With the awl, make a small hole at each dot. Use a hole punch to punch the Rabbit's eye.
4. The Cat and Rabbit Chairs work fine unpainted, but the Flower needs to be colored or painted to make visual sense.
5. On the first chair sides, put a dab of hot glue in the pierced holes. Push the dowels into the holes.

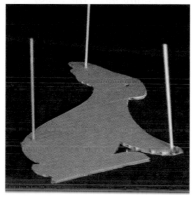

The dowels are glued to one side of the chair.

6. The dowels are pointing up in the air. Put a dab of hot glue in each of the holes on the other chair side and push the ends of the dowels into place in the holes. Correct any wobbles now and add more hot glue around the dowel ends if necessary.

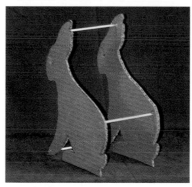

The dowels are glued to the other side.

7. The finished size of the seat needs to be 4" by 12". Either weave the seat, finish fabric edges, or crochet one to arrive at the finished dimensions (see below).

8. Lay the fabric, woven, or crocheted seat over the dowel at the front of the chair, taking about 1" around to the underside of the chair. Stitch or glue the fabric in place. Fold the other end of the fabric over the upper dowel. Pin in place. Try several of your dolls out in the chair. If their feet don't touch the ground, pull more fabric over the back of the chair. When you are happy with the "sling" of the seat, stitch or glue it in place.

Gluing the lower edge to the seat. Don't glue the upper edge until you're sure how much "sling" you want in the seat.

Materials and Tools for the Fabric Seat (not shown)

6" by 14" piece of fabric
Sewing machine needle and thread, or hot glue gun and sticks
Scissors
Ruler
Iron and ironing board

1. Turn 1/4" under on all edges of fabric. Press.
2. Either sew or glue edges in place.
3. Sew or glue seat to chair, wrapping and gluing ends around dowels.

Materials and Tools for the Woven Seat

1 ball worsted weight "dish-
  cloth" yarn (approx. 2 oz.)*
Lap Loom A, pin board
  loom**, or Weavette Loom 4"
  by 6" size***
Optional: shed stick
Optional: shuttle
Darning needle
Ruler
Scissors

*Used in this project: *The Rabbit Chair has a seat woven from Lily Sugar'n Cream #201, Jewels, #01 White, and #2 Black. The Flower Chair has a seat woven from the wool that comes with the Lap Loom A.*

**For a pin board loom, you will need a piece of dense foam or insulation board that's 6" by 14". You will also need a 6" by 14" piece of 1/4" graph paper and thirty-four pins. Place the paper on the board. Insert seventeen pins 1" from the lower edge, every 1/4". Insert seventeen pins 1" from the upper edge, every 1/4". This will give you the finished dimensions of 4" by 12" for your weaving.*

***If using a Weavette Loom, weave two rectangles and sew them together along a 4" edge to make a 4" by 12" piece.*

The finished size of the weaving needs to be 4" by 12".

Materials and Tools for the Crocheted Seat

1 ball worsted weight "dish-
  cloth" yarn (approx. 2 oz.)*
Crochet hook, G, B, or 4mm**
Scissors
Ruler

*Used in this project: The Cat Chair has a seat that is crocheted in Afghan or Tunisian stitch, but single crochet will work fine. *I crocheted them in Lily Sugar'n Cream #164 Flair and #196 Very Berry. I worked fifteen st for forty-one rows on a 4mm hook; **I used an afghan-type hook, which is extra long, for one of the seats, and a Brittany Wooden hook for one of them to see if an afghan hook is necessary. It's not if your hook has a long enough shaft without a finger grip.*

Tunisian or Afghan Stitch Seat

1. Ch 16.
2. Skip first ch. * Insert hook through next ch, yo over hook, draw loop of yarn through ch, and leave it on your hook * repeat along row. You will have sixteen loops on your hook. Do not turn.
3. Yo, draw yarn through first loop on hook. * yo, draw through two loops * repeat to end of row (1 loop on hook). Do not turn.
4. Ch 1, * insert hook from the right to the left through the vertical st on the front of the previous row, draw up a loop * across row (16 loops on hook—15 st in row). Do not turn. Repeat rows 3 and 4 until seat is 12" long. (I worked rows 3 and 4 twenty times.)

Single Crochet Seat

1. Ch 16.
2. Sc in second ch from hook * sc across row, ch 1, turn * (15sc) repeat until seat is 12" long.

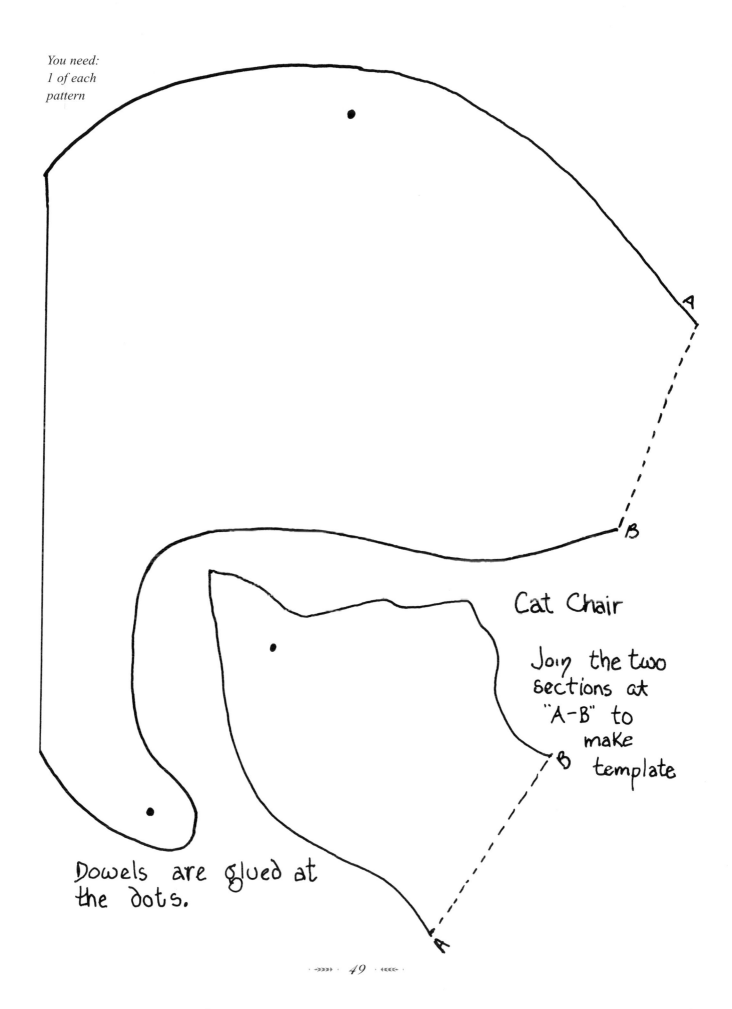

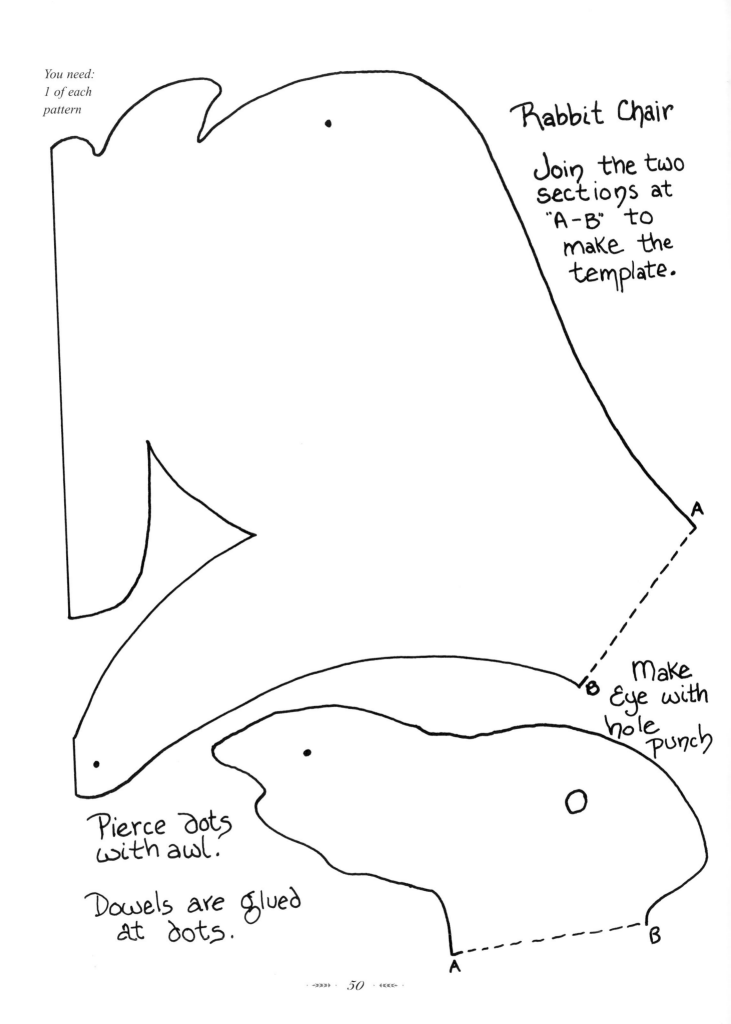

You need:
1 of each
pattern

Rabbit Chair

Join the two
sections at
"A-B" to
make the
template.

A

B

Make
Eye with
hole
Punch

O

Pierce dots
with awl.

Dowels are glued
at dots.

A

B

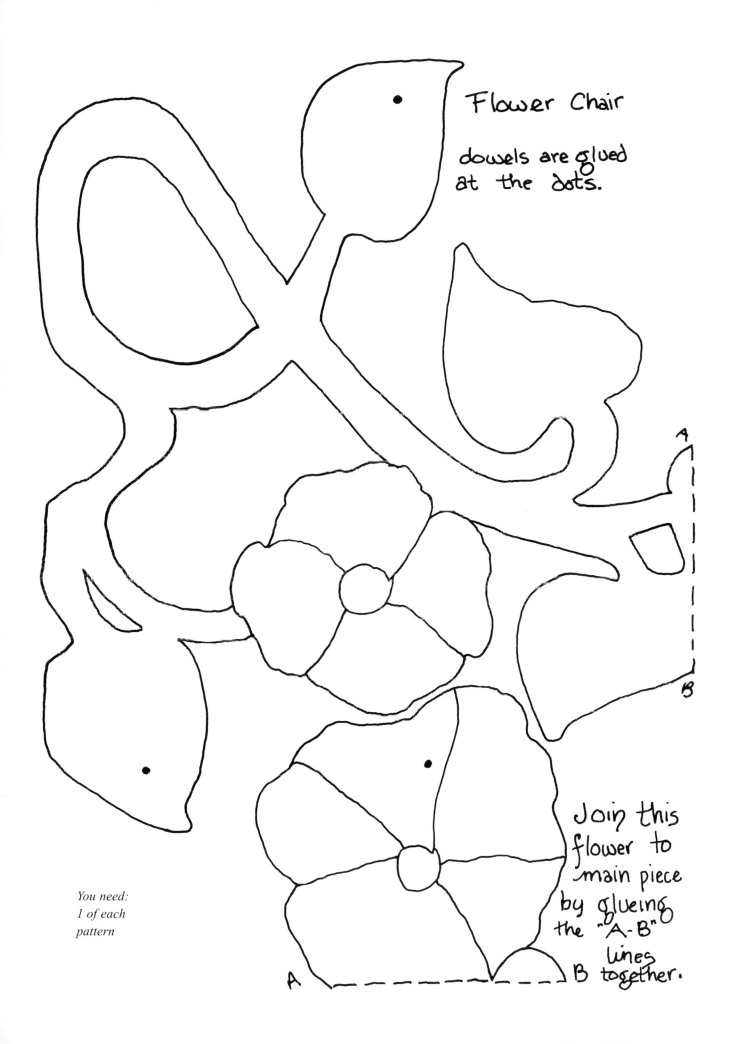

Flower Chair

dowels are glued at the dots.

A

B

You need:
1 of each
pattern

Join this flower to main piece by glueing the "A-B" lines together.

A - - - - - - - - - - - - - B

3 chapter

Journal Work, Coloring Pages, Dreamwork, and Doodling

Various types of journals.

A journal is a powerful tool that helps us make sense of our lives. Writing in a journal is a great way of working through dilemmas. It is also perfect for recording exciting or gratifying events, insights, and other precious elements that need to be remembered.

A journal gives clarity and meaning to our lives. It helps us cultivate wisdom and discernment. It's a place to record the neat things that you hear or read, things that will help you live a better life; I call mine an Inspiration File. But now, I'm going to introduce you to a different kind of journal keeping. It's very simple and astonishingly powerful.

First, buy yourself a couple of small notebooks and some cray-ons (preferably fat ones). Next, at some point in the day, take 5 minutes for yourself. You're going to start your Coloring Pages, a different kind of journal.

Why would I ask you to start a different kind of journal? Because I am going to ask you to take a brief holiday from words. Words are wonderful, but we live in a sea of words. We are bombarded with them, and sometimes they can keep us in our heads and out of our hearts.

So, I am going to ask you to play with color. I asked you to buy fat crayons because I want you to use **fat** color. Forget stingy, skinny little lines. Especially at first, I want you to work in swooping, flailing, wide strokes. Color drops you right into feeling.

Here's an exercise: "What color was my day?"

Find a color that matches the predominant mood or feeling tone of the day. Color some of that shade and then add touches of other colors that might have entered your day. A lovely, lyric, relaxed day will have different colors than a frantically busy, rush rush omigosh day. When you have a lousy fug-filled day, full of squelcher voices, what color does that feel like? I bet it isn't pretty. I bet it's muddy, smooshed, has heavy colors, and is downright ugh ugly. Good. Fill up a page or two in your little notebook with those yech colors. Maybe try some other colors on for size as antidotes and then go on to the next exercise.

You might like to put on some instrumental music for the next exercise: Imagine that the music is singing a song without words, and the different voices are each a different color. Give each

Minnaloushe sleeps among the Coloring Pages.

voice a color. Swirl the colors around. Use the sides of your crayons. Move with the colors of their conversation. Is it light and skippety, or solemn and stately? What happens to the colors and the strokes when the music speeds up or slows down? What happens to the colors and strokes when the music gets choppy or smooth and lyrical?

The Coloring Pages are not always so involved. Often it's just asking yourself the question "What colors do I feel like right now?" Or you might find that one particular part of your body has your attention. What colors does it feel like? Do you want that feeling to change? If so, what colors would you like it to feel like? Are any shapes being repeated? Neat. Enjoy them.

Your homework is this: A minimum of three (yes, three— that's why I asked you to get a small notebook. Little pages will only take moments.) Coloring Pages a day. Start with a feeling

tone and put that into colors. Try to be there for a sunrise or sunset and put those colors into your Coloring Pages.

When a difficult situation arises, go to your Coloring Pages. Color in a shape that expresses how you feel right now. Color what the problem is. Then color how you want to feel about the problem, imagining that it is already resolved.

As you keep working daily with the Coloring Pages, you will find that images start to emerge. You will start to build a vocabulary of those images.

If you have a squelcher inside you that says, "You can't draw!" you know what to say—a great big "Pah Shaw!" This is not about drawing at all; this is about learning to see your life in new ways.

If your squelcher lets you have it for "wasting" paper, then assure the squelcher that you will find other ways to be a good earthkeeper. By all means, keep that promise!

The Coloring Pages are like a butterfly net. You catch the flitting emotions and thought patterns in the colors, examine them, and let go of them. In this way, the Coloring Pages teach us discernment and give us a process that filters information.

Soon, Soul Mate Dolls will begin to suggest themselves. My Coloring Pages often evolve—that's where the Ancient Dancer Soul Mate Dolls came from.

Ancient Dancer Soul Mate Doll

Materials and Tools

3.5mm knitting needles for fine yarns*; use 4.5mm knitting needles for heavy yarns**
Row counter
Ruler to sit on the graph, above the row you are presently knitting
Darning needle
Stuffing
Scissors
Small clamp

*Used in this project: *1 ball (approx. 3.5 oz.) Bernat Aspen Textured Neps yarn in Natural; **2 strands held together of Berella Muskoka 9838 Denims.*

1. Body: Repeat the body chart twice to make a front and a back. Cast on 25 st and follow the chart from row 1 to row 75. Cut yarn and pull end through.

2. Base (make 1): Cast on 11 st and follow the base chart from row 1 to row 12.

3. Arms (make 2): Cast on 3 st and follow the chart from row 1 to row 28. The arm will naturally curl in on itself, so you don't need to sew it up. Weave the end from the finger tips into the inside of the arm.

4. Finishing: With your darning needle, sew the body front to the back, starting at one shoulder. When you have sewn across one shoulder and up and over the head and down the second side of the neck, stop and stuff the head. Push tiny bits of stuffing into head with the knitting needle.

5. Sew across the second shoulder and down one side. Sew the second side. Sew the base to the lower body edge, leaving an opening for stuffing. Stuff. Sew shut. Sew the arms

to the body at the shoulder.

6. Hair: Cut nine 16" lengths of yarn. Wrap a short length of yarn around the ends several times, then tie and knot it. Clamp the tied end to the table. Divide the yarn into groups of three strands and braid them. Wrap the ends with another length of yarn, tie, and knot. Clip close to the ends.

7. Starting at the center of the head, at eyebrow level, stitch the center of the braid to the head. At the side of the head, make a coil. Pin in place and stitch. Repeat with the other end of the braid on the other side of the head. Cross the cord at the back of the head, twirl, and wrap the braid around the head to complete the hairstyle. Stitch in place.

How to Read a Knitting Chart

It looks intimidating, but really it's not. The doll is basically worked in stockinet stitch (one row knit, one row purl). Each square represents one stitch. The empty squares indicate knitting on the right side and purling on the wrong side. Squares with codes or marks are instructing you to do something else. Check the key to see what the marked squares mean. The rows are numbered starting at bottom right. The odd-numbered rows are knit and the even rows are purled. The right side is the knit side, the wrong side is the purl side. When the chart moves in, decrease the number of stitches represented by the number of squares. When the chart moves out, increase that number of stitches.

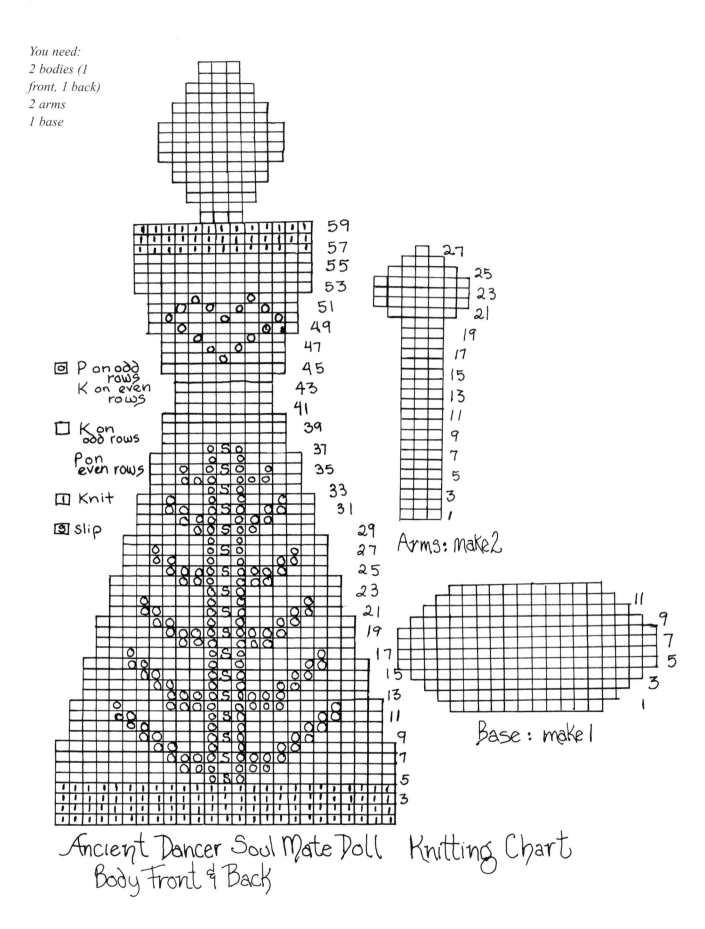

You need:
2 bodies (1 front, 1 back)
2 arms
1 base

59
57
55
53
51
49
47
45
43
41
39
37
35
33
31
29
27
25
23
21
19
17
15
13
11
9
7
5
3

☑ P on odd rows
  K on even rows

☐ K on odd rows
  P on even rows

Ⅰ Knit

Ⓢ Slip

27
25
23
21
19
17
15
13
11
9
7
5
3
1

Arms: make 2

11
9
7
5
3
1

Base: make 1

Ancient Dancer Soul Mate Doll Knitting Chart
Body Front & Back

Circle of Song Dancer Soul Mate Dolls

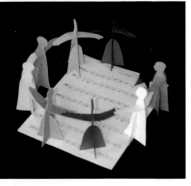

Dancers keep showing up in my Coloring Pages. They are very simply shaped and colorful. I call these the Circle of Song Dancers. Each one stands alone, but when two or more are together, they seem to dance a dance of healing and peace.

Materials and Tools

Brightly-colored wrapping or origami paper or acrylic paints and paintbrush
Card stock (because this doll is fairly small, lightweight card stock works fine)
Sharp craft knife
Cutting mat
Scissors
Gluo
Hot glue gun and sticks

1. Copy doll pattern and glue it to card stock.
2. Glue colored paper to or paint the other side of the card stock. Let dry.
3. Cut out doll.
4. Glue colored paper to or paint the first side of doll so that it is now colored on both sides. When paint or glue is dry, cut out the doll pieces.
5. The notches are best if they fit together tightly, so cut them very narrow and keep checking for fit. When you are happy with the fit, run a line of hot glue along the joint to seal them in place.

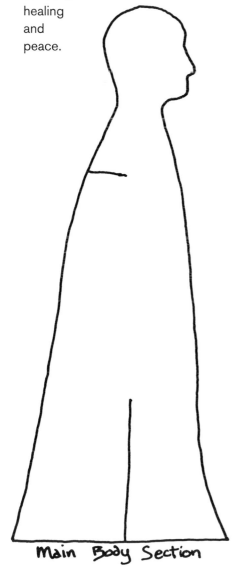

Main Body Section

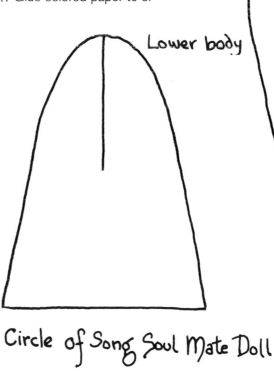

Lower body

Circle of Song Soul Mate Doll

arms

You need: 1 of each pattern

Another Way of Using the Coloring Pages

I meet so many people who are simply "numbed out"— exhausted and depleted by the demands of their lives. Something has dried up and the doorway to creativity has slammed shut. They can't even imagine having a passion, let alone soaring to the heights of discovery with it. What can you do if you find yourself in this state?

First of all, you commit yourself to taking a few minutes whenever, wherever, and as often as you can to "change that dial." If your TV or radio is tuned to a channel that doesn't offer you good things, you change channels. Well, you can do that in your life, as well.

Speaking of the TV and radio, turn them off while you're metaphorically changing your channels. Turn off the computer, push away that magazine, unplug the phone. Get your notebook and ask yourself "What if....?," "Why?," "What does this mean?," and "How could this be different?" Write one of these questions out, and then grab your crayons and color, color, color before you start to write.

Now, let a word or phrase pop up in your mind. Print it in the middle of a clean page and color a shape around it. For one minute, pour out all of the words that the word(s) in the middle bring up.

Take a crayon and draw a line from the center out to the words that seem to be the most important. These lines are your "One Hair Bridges" (see The Story of Molly Whuppie, page 34).

Turn the page again and choose some of the bridged words or phrases to write on this new page. Try writing them in colors, or doodling animals and plants around them. As you move around the words and the colors, you might begin to feel things shifting inside yourself. If you do this regularly, you will develop new skills and find the doorway to creativity slowly but surely opening to you.

Dreamwork

Do you have trouble remembering your dreams? There are ways of training yourself to remember them. Before you go to sleep, quietly, but firmly, assure yourself that you can indeed remember your dreams.

It is time to make friends with the Dream Spinner. Imagine that there is a lovely woman whose joy it is to spin wonderful, meaning-filled dreams for you. Welcome her into your life and ask her to start by spinning up a simple dream that you will be able to catch and hold onto. Decide to wake up as soon as you finish a dream. Simply tell yourself that you will. Then, immediately grab a notebook and write down or sketch anything you remember from the dream like a feeling tone, smell, texture, sound, sequence of movements, or a fragment of a story line. These are keys that the Dream Spinner is leaving for you. She wants you to be able to use the wisdom and information she's weaving up for you. Keep at it. Perseverance and commitment are vital to the process.

Gradually, you will remember more and more of your dreams. Some of them are junk, so just toss them into your metaphorical dream trash can. Some of them are terrifying. In this case, firmly state, "This dream will not come true, anytime, anywhere, to anyone, for any reason!" You may need to check out if there is something in your waking world that *is* actually a threat. If there is, thank the Dream Spinner for pointing this out to you, and for goodness sake, take action to correct the situation.

Your dreams can give you incredible insights. They can help you understand aspects of your waking life by giving you another perspective on it. Working with your dreams will most definitely increase your "creativity quotient." Your dreams will influence your waking world once you get in the habit of working with them. Phrases from dreams can become catchwords for you, reminding you of a particularly wise or delightful moment in a dream. Repeating it can bring that lesson right into the present moment.

Much of my work is based on my dreams. I make many Soul Mate Dolls that have been gifts from the Dream Spinner. Making and then living with the dolls is very important. It keeps me in touch with the wonderful world of dreams and all of its possibilities and potential. When I see the dolls, they rekindle the power of the dream.

Recently, I had a really special dream in which two friends helped me climb an invisible flight of stairs. They said, "Fly!" and so I did! It was so much fun! This dream told me in no uncertain terms to *trust*!

I made the Soaring Soul Mate Doll to celebrate this dream. I hope she will inspire you to soar in your life and dreams, as well! She is made using the Basic Flat Doll technique (page 11), except that, like the Circle of Song Dancers, she is notched. She hangs from a strand of monofilament that is strung through the hole in her hair.

Soaring Soul Mate Doll

Materials and Tools

Gold wrapping paper or gold
  paint and paintbrush
Card stock (because this doll
  is small, fairly lightweight
  card stock works fine)
Monofilament thread
Sharp craft knife
Cutting mat
Awl
Scissors
Glue
Hot glue gun and sticks

1. Copy the pattern and glue it
to card stock.
2. Glue gold wrapping paper to
the other side of the card stock.
Let dry. (See Step 4 if you are
painting the doll.)
3. Cut out doll. Pierce a hole in
the hair.
4. Glue gold wrapping paper to
the first side of the doll so that it
is now gold on both sides. If you
are painting the doll, paint both
sides now. When the paint or
glue is dry, cut out the doll
pieces.

5. The notches are best if they fit
together tightly, so cut them very
narrow and keep checking for fit.
When you are happy with the fit,
run a line of hot glue under the
arm at the joint to seal it.
6. Thread monofilament thread
through the hole in the hair.
Make a loop at the other end
and tie it in a knot so that you
can hang up the doll.

You need:
1 of each
pattern

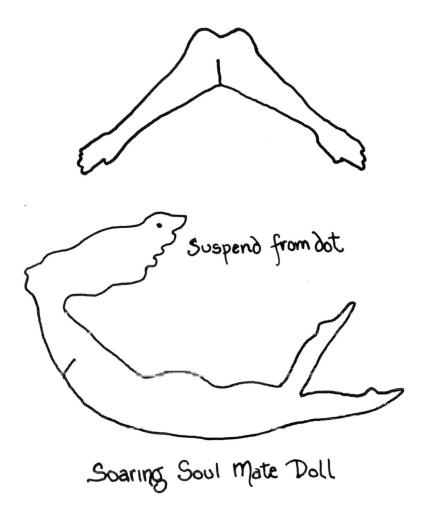

Suspend from dot

Soaring Soul Mate Doll

The Skater's Dream

Another dream that has been really significant for me was about skaters on a frozen river. In the dream, there were many, many skaters skating on a river that had been cleared of snow. There were, however, holes in the ice.

Most of the skaters seemed to be skating rapidly in one direction, although occasionally some would skate against the flow of traffic. Almost all of the skaters seemed to be able to avoid each other and the holes in the ice, but sometimes one would fall through the hole to the icy water. When other skaters would try to assist the fallen skater, sometimes they would get pulled into the ice, too. This would have a variety of outcomes. Others were able to assist without getting pulled in.

It was exhilarating to watch the masterful skaters flying along, who were not only able to avoid the holes in the ice, but who were able to leap, twirl, and fly over and around them. This dream still has tremendous energy for me, in the power of its metaphor about choices in living. I have made a lot of Skater Soul Mate Dolls since having this dream and am including directions for you to make one, too.

Skater Soul Mate Doll

Use the Skater/Joyous Dancer Pattern to make a pin board for bending the armature of the doll. I used chenille stems for this doll, but 20-gauge wire works, too.

Materials and Tools

Chenille stems or 20-gauge wire
Crochet cotton and embroidery floss*
Small rectangle of skin-tone fabric
Charms**
Stuffing
Hot glue gun and glue sticks
Paper

A piece of sturdy foam or insulation board or acoustical ceiling tile
Pins
Embroidery floss***
2.25mm knitting needles****
Needlenose pliers
Row counter (paper and pencil will do)
Dowel or paintbrush, approximately 3/4" in diameter
Darning needle
Scissors

Wire snips

*Used in this project: *Bernat Handicrafter Crochet Cotton, size 10, Ecru; **"Winter Time" silver charms from Birdhouse Enterprises; ***Watercolours Charcoal from the Caron Collection; ****Six-strand Igolochkoy embroidery needle for the vest.*

1. Copy the pattern. Place it on the pin board and push pins in at each of the numbered dots. For this doll you will not make the heart base, so do not push pins into the heart section.

2. Body: Using chenille stems or wire, follow the numbered path around the jig, beginning with #13 (#1). Twist chenille stems or wire together to join them. Skip the thumbs, because you will knit mittens that will have thumbs. Lift the doll off the armature. Read the instructions in the Joyous Dancer Doll (page 68) for an explanation of the "locking" process.

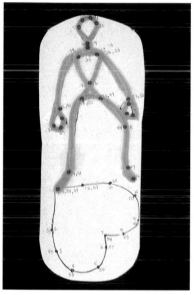

Making the "skeleton" for the Skater Soul Mate Doll with chenille stems by following the numbers on the pin board.

3. Reinforce the torso by wrapping an extra chenille stem or piece or wire around the hips, twisting it around the waist and through and around the shoulders.

4. Reinforce the legs by twisting another chenille stem or piece of wire around the first leg, starting at the toe, up the leg, across the hips, and down the second leg.

5. Head: Scrunch up a small wad of paper and put it into the open space of the head. Starting at the chin, wrap another chenille stem or piece of wire around the head. Turn the head so that the "outline" becomes the center front and back. Glue the rectangle of fabric to the head, smoothing out any wrinkles as you go. Depending on the weight of your fabric, you may want to put a thin layer of stuffing on the head first. Trim excess fabric.

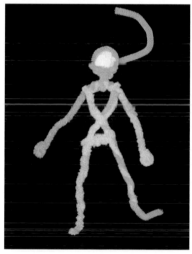

The Skater's head is stuffed and the chenille stem is being wrapped around it.

6. Sweater: Using two strands of crochet cotton and 2.25mm needles,
a. Sleeves:
Make two: Cast on 10 st and work 25 rows in st st. Cast off.
Front and Back: Cast on 13 st and work 30 rows in st st. Cast off.
b. Assembling: Place sleeves on arms and sew underarm seam. Place front and back of sweater on doll. Sew shoulder seam. Sew upper edge of sleeves to front and back. Sew side seams. Put a little stuffing inside torso.

7. Legs: Wrap thin strips of stuffing around legs to shape

them. Glue skates to feet. (Here, the skates are the Winter Time charms.)

8. Leggings:
Using one skein of embroidery floss (six strands) and 2.25mm needles,
Make two beginning at toe:
R. 1 - 10: Cast on 9 st and work in st st.
R. 11: Inc 1 st at each end.
R. 12: Purl.
R. 13 - 16: Repeat rows 11 and 12 twice. (13 st).
R. 17 - 51: Work in st st. Cast off.
Glue foot of leggings to doll's foot. Sew center back seam.

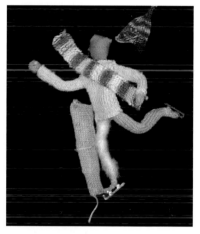

Assembling the Skater.

9. Hat: Using 2.25mm knitting needles and one skein of embroidery floss, make two earflaps:
Cast on 2 st.
R. 1: K 2.
R. 2: P 2.
R. 3 and 5: Increase one stitch at each end of the row.
R. 4 and 6: Purl.
Cut yarn. Place on a stitch holder (a pin or a spare needle).
R. 7: Cast on two stitches, knit across one ear flap, cast on nine stitches, knit across second flap, cast on two stitches.
R. 8 - 18: work in st st on these

25 st.

R. 19 - 30: repeat the following 4 rows 3 times from * to *:

R. 1: k 2 tog to last st, k 1

R. 2: p

R. 3: k

R. 4: p

Cut yarn, pull through remaining stitches, and sew center back seam. Weave in any loose ends. Glue to doll's head.

10. Scarf: Using 2.25mm knitting needles and one skein of embroidery floss, cast on seven stitches and knit 100 rows. Cast off. Weave in ends. Glue in place around neck.

11. Mittens: Using 2.25mm knitting needles and one skein of embroidery floss,

Cast on ten stitches and work ten rows st st.

Next row: K 2 tog. across row. Purl one row.

Cut yarn and draw through remaining five stitches. At the fifth row, in the center of the mitten, pick up three stitches. Work three rows st st on these three stitches.

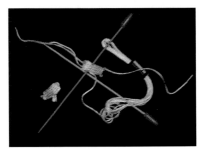

The Skater's mittens.

Cut yarn, draw through 3 st. Sew thumb seam, take yarn ends through to wrong side of mitten, and tie off.

Sew side seam, slide mitten onto hand, sew mitten cuff to sleeve edge.

12. Vest: This vest is made the same way as the Vest for the Gatekeeper Soul Mate Doll (page 32). The only difference is that I separated the three strands of Watercolours thread from Caron and used one strand in the six-strand Igolochkoy needle. If you use regular embroidery floss, use the full six strands of floss in the 6-strand needle. I sewed the snowflake charms onto the vest after it was assembled.

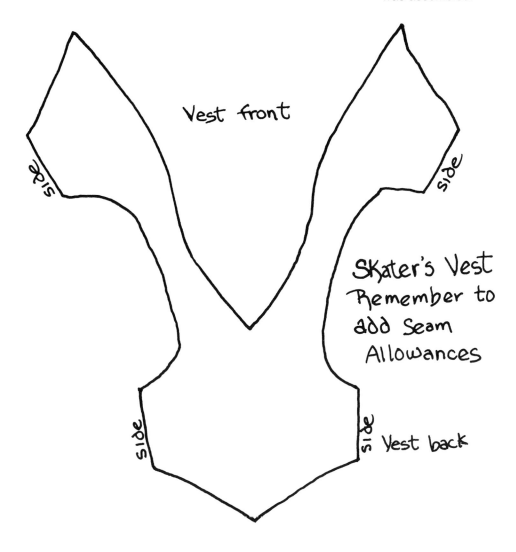

Vest front

side

side

Skater's Vest
Remember to
add Seam
Allowances

side

side Vest back

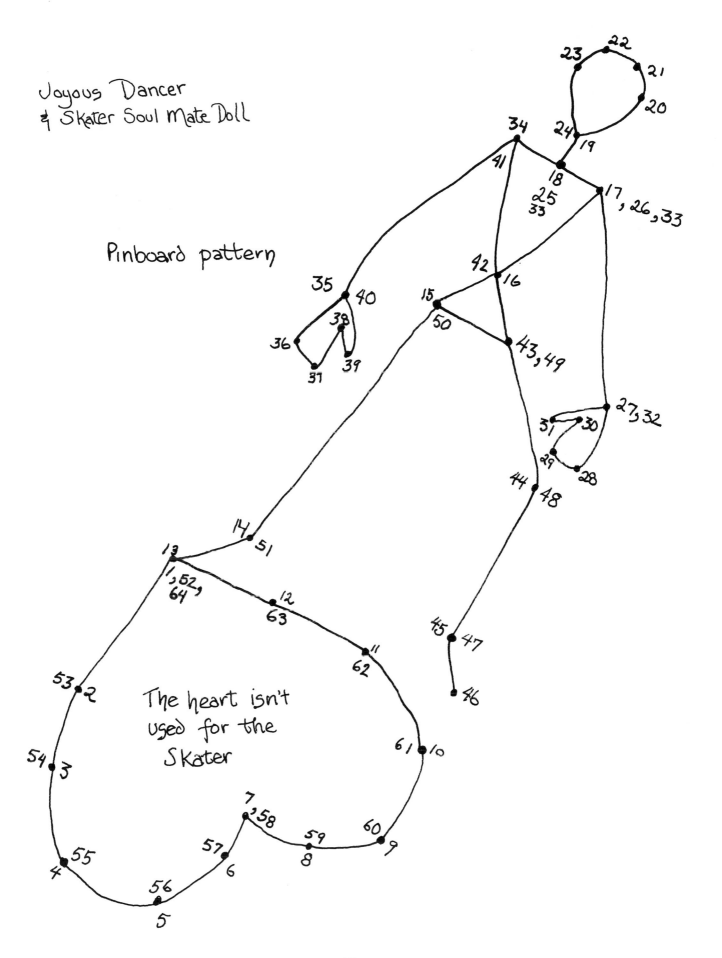

Joyous Dancer
& Skater Soul mate Doll

Pinboard pattern

The heart isn't
used for the
Skater

Daydreaming is very important! The Dream Spinner can actively inspire you when you daydream, offering you delightful new ways of being the creative wonder you were meant to be! You might not reinvent quantum mechanics in your daydreams, but allowing yourself a moment or two of daydreaming time can invigorate and refresh you.

When the creative well is full to over-flowing, it's so important to catch as much of the flow as possible. Little notes to yourself and the most fleeting of thumbnail sketches are the source of incredible pleasure in those times when the well feels dry.

The little doodles and noodlings are treasures; they can open the door to creativity when it feels like it has slammed shut forever. By taking a few seconds to catch thoughts and images on paper, you are giving yourself a source book of inspiration that is uniquely your own.

Doodling

I highly recommend that you keep a pile of paper beside the phone. When you're chatting, let the tip of the pen wander and meander over the paper. You'll probably find that you have a repertoire of doodle patterns. Use these to "dress" a Flat Soul Mate Doll, to remind you of the riches that lie just below the surface of your mind.

Often, people will doodle "stick people." It's possible to lift the stick people right up off the paper and let them dance with joy! You do this by making Joyous Dancer Wire Soul Mate Dolls.

Joyous Dancer Wire
Soul Mate Doll

The Joyous Dancer Wire Soul Mate Doll has a heart-shaped base (see the pattern on page 65). This is because love builds the strongest foundation for a well-lived life. When you make several Joyous Dancers, you can join their bases by threading the wire through them. The overlapping hearts make lovely patterns. A group of Joyous Dancers is a perfect illustration of a harmonious community, which is definitely something for us all to aspire to.

If you choose to make the Joyous Dancers larger, you will need heavier wire and 1-1/2" nails pounded into plywood for the armature.

Materials and Tools

Spool of 24-gauge wire
Needlenose pliers with a
   cutting notch
Box of short, straight pins
Pin board
Pen
Pencil or paintbrush, 3/4" in
   diameter

1. Copy the pattern. Place it on the pin board and push pins in at each of the numbered dots.
2. Leaving a 1" tail of wire, and starting at pin #1, follow the numbered path. Some of the dots have several numbers. This is because you will be coming back to that dot in sequence. Sometimes, you will pass on one side of a pin and the other side of the next one in order to make the wire take the right shape. When you reach #13, twist the tail around the working wire to lock it.
3. You have made the first pass around the base. At the end, you will pass around the base again. Now, follow the path of the dots around the outline of the body. Be sure to maintain the continuity of the number sequence.
4. When you are back at #1 (#63), twist the wire around the beginning tail. Do not cut the wire off yet.

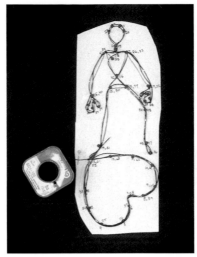

Wrapping the wire to make the Joyous Dancer.

5. Right hand and arm: Pull out **only** pins #35, 36, 37, 38, and 39. Being careful to not pull out the shoulder pins, put a pen through the hand and twist the arm. Push the wires at the shoulder down with the finger of your other hand and turn the pen approximately twenty times.
6. Repeat Step 6 for the left, pulling out pins #27, 28, 29, 30, and 31.
7. Pull out pins #18, 19, 20, 21, 22, and 23. Hold the three wires that form the left shoulder together with the needlenose pliers. Put the pencil or paintbrush through the head and twist the neck three or four times to shape the neck and lock the head.
8. Push the right arm through the chest a few times to lock it.
9. Pull out pin #17. Push the head through the chest and twist it a few times to lock the shoulders completely.
10. Push down with your fingers at the waist and twist the

upper body a few times to lock it.
11 . Left leg: Pull out pins #43, 44, 45, and 46. Hold down the hip at #43. Put a pen through the foot and twist twenty times.
12. Pull the pins out of the base, as well as #14 and 15.
13. Feed the spool of wire in and out of the base of the heart, wrapping the heart to make it sturdy.
14. Put a pen through the foot at the base of the heart. Lay the doll on the pattern to establish where #15 is. Pinch the hip wires here. Allowing the base to flap around, turn the pen twenty times to lock this leg.

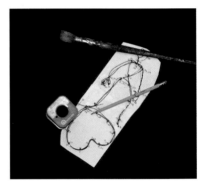

Using a pencil and paintbrush to twist the head and hands to lock them into position.

15. Shape the doll into a pleasing position. Practice a few of her joyous dance moves yourself! Make her a community to dance with.

Doodle Fairy Soul Mate Doll

When I went rummaging through old sketchbooks looking for the original doodles for the Doodle Fairy, I was delighted. So many ideas for Soul Mate Dolls! And I had forgotten them all. Thank heavens I had taken a moment to jot them down!

Materials and Tools

Card stock
Plain paper
2 paper clips (plastic-covered
  to match dress)
Sharp craft knife
Cutting mat
Scissors
Needlenose pliers
Permanent black felt-tip
  marker
Vanishing ink marker or pencil
Colored pencils, crayons,
  markers, or acrylic paints and
  paintbrush
Awl
Hot glue gun and sticks
Glue
Monofilament thread
Paper clip
Wire snips

1. Copy the pattern.

2. Glue the patterns to the card stock.

3. When completely dry, cut out the pieces, leaving a small margin around them. Glue plain paper to the "wrong" side. When completely dry, cut out the pieces along the lines. Both sides of the card stock are now covered with paper.

4. Paint the edges of all of the pieces.

5. Now for the doodles: You can snip up and glue on your favorite doodles, or you can just let your mind and fingers wander and doodle freeform right on your Doodle Fairy. Use whatever pens, pencils, crayons, or paints that appeal to you. Be sure that both sides of the arms are colored.

6. Pierce holes at the shoulder of the body and upper arms and at the elbows.

7. Make wire joints for each elbow. (See Basic Flat Doll instructions, page 13.) There is just one joint for the shoulder. Push the joint wire through the shoulder hole on one upper arm and then through the body. Push the second arm onto the wire and twist into a loop. Flatten the loop with the pliers to lock. Be sure that all three joints (two elbow and one shoulder) are tightly squeezed so they can hold the position you place them in.

8. The Doodle Fairy can hold a treasure in her hands, if you wish.

9. Glue the wings in place, being sure that they don't impede the arms' movement.

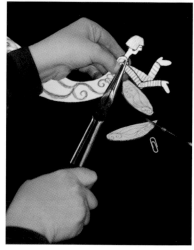

Making the shoulder joints for the Doodle Fairy Soul Mate Doll.

10. Hanger: To find the doll's balance point, lightly hold her wings with your thumb and fore-finger. Move along the upper edge of the wing, until she hangs level. Mark this spot with a vanishing ink marker or pencil. Now, cut about 1" from a paper clip and bend it in half. Squeeze a dab of hot glue between the wings at the balance point. Push the ends of the wire loop into the hot glue. String monofil-ament thread through the wire loop and hang her up.

You need:
1 of each pattern

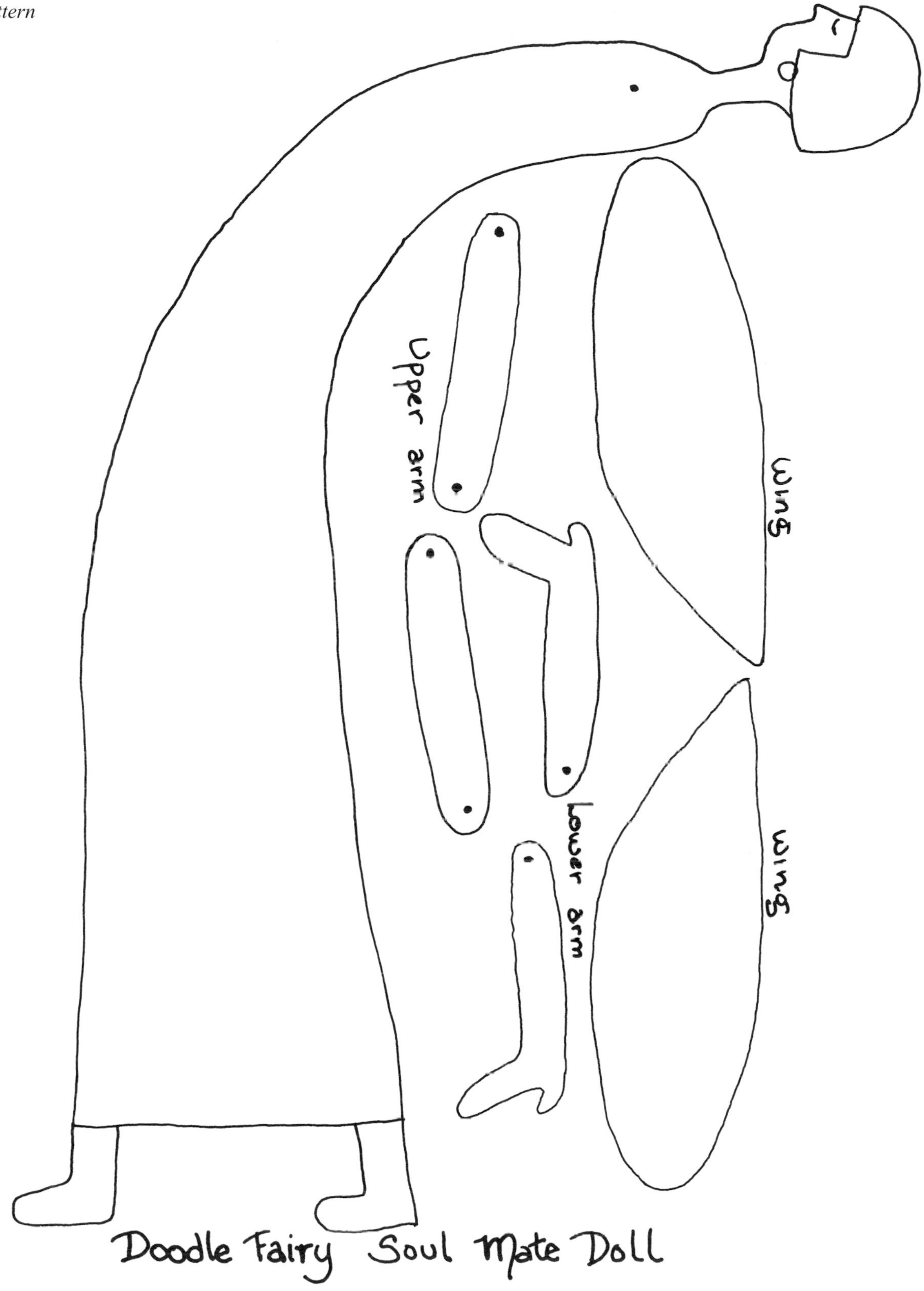
Upper arm
Wing
Lower arm
Wing
Doodle Fairy Soul Mate Doll

4 chapter

Emotions and Feelings

Emotions are an incredibly important part of human existence. We can use Soul Mate Dollmaking to help us heal and release painful, difficult, or negative emotions and experiences. We can also be inspired through remembrance and celebration of positive experiences and emotions. We can aspire to achieve even more positive feeling states and experiences by making Soul Mate Dolls that are the embodiment of those longed-for states.

When I think about the power of aspiring to move feelings to a more positive state, I think about the ability we have to change our minds. Changing our minds changes how we feel, and that changes our whole life.

For instance, I was recently forced to drive through a blizzard on icy roads. The wind was tearing at the car, there were awful accidents all around me, and I was in a state of terror and dread. But, that morning, when I had been contemplating the awful necessity of venturing out into the horrors of

the weather, I had suddenly been inspired to make a new Soul Mate Doll. The doll was called Changing Channels. She had a dial in her magnificently robust tummy that allowed her to sample all of the colors of the rainbow, rather than staying in the gray or polarized black and white.

As I negotiated the roads, simply calling up her image in my mind reminded me of my options: fall apart and end up a weeping heap in the ditch, or summon up my alertness and attention and get home safely. I opted for the latter, continually assuring myself that my guardian angel was on duty, and I got home just fine. (Exhausted, but intact.)

Needless to say, I am now very attached to this Soul Mate Doll, and want to share her with you.

Changing Channels Soul Mate Doll

Materials and Tools

11" by 17" piece of medium-
  weight card stock
Curly pot scrubber
Wooden knob, button, or plug
  for her tummy "control" (I
  used a wooden button that is
  used to cover countersunk
  screws, 1/2" diameter by
  3/8" high.)
Optional: buttons and charms
Sharp craft knife
Paints and paintbrush, cray-
  ons, or colored pencils
Hot glue gun and glue sticks
Craft glue
Needlenose pliers
Awl
18-gauge wire or plastic-
  covered paper clips
Wire snips
24" of black bias tape
2 small clamps
Scissors
Compass and ruler

1. Copy the patterns. Copy the color wheel pattern onto white paper. Color it and glue it to card stock. When completely dry, cut out.
2. Trace the body, arms, and legs onto card stock. Trace the

The parts of the Changing Channels Soul Mate Doll.

outline of the body onto card stock for the body back. Glue the patterns onto card stock.
3. When dry, cut out the body front and back, arms, and legs. With the awl, pierce holes at the dots. Glue paper to the back of the arms and legs and allow to dry; then cut away excess.

4. Trace around the base of the wooden button at the circle on the doll's tummy. Cut out this circle.

Cut out the circle and color the wheel window.

5. Cut out the window on the tummy, being sure to leave at least a 1/4" between it and the button circle hole.

6. Color or paint the dress, shoes, and stockings, both front and back.

7. Place the exact center of the color wheel at the exact center of the button hole. Put a dab of glue on the bottom center of the button and glue it to the color wheel, being very careful to not get any glue on the doll's dress. Let the glue dry. It really helps to make the mechanism stronger by putting a dab of glue on a thumbtack and pushing it into the center of the circle from the back. (I've had the button pull off in my hand when turning the wheel–very frustrating.) Make sure that when you turn the button, the color wheel moves freely behind the dress. The colors will change in the window.

Gluing the wooden button to the color wheel (tricky!).

8. With the compass, draw fourteen 1" diameter circles on card stock. Cut them out and slightly enlarge the hole at the center of each. These circles will act as spacers that allow the color wheel to move freely inside the body.

9. Cut four pieces of wire or paper clip, each approximately 2" long. Make a loop at one end of each wire.

10. Push the wire through the hole in the arm shoulder, then through the body, then through the three cardboard circles. Repeat with the other arm. The loops are on the outside of the body.

Making the arm joint for the Changing Channels Doll.

11. Push another wire through one hole in the hem of her skirt. Put two card stock circles on the wire, against the inside of the body, then the leg, then another two circles. Repeat with the other leg.

Making the leg joint for the Changing Channels Doll.

12. Trace the head shape onto card stock twice and cut out. Glue these inside the doll's head.

Gluing the head for the Changing Channels Doll.

13. Push wires through the appropriate holes in back of body, put glue on the inside of the back of the head, and push the body front and back together. Clamp the edges of the head.

14. With the needlenose pliers, make loops in the ends of the wires on the back of the body. Fold over the loops on the front and back of the body, being sure that the loops are both folded in the same direction. Squeeze shut.

Close the loops on the back of the doll.

15. Glue bias tape to the front and back edges, all around her body, to cover the gap.

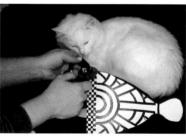
Minnaloushe supervises gluing bias tape around the edges of the Changing Channels Doll.

16. Pull the pot scrubber into wild and wonderful shapes and glue it on the doll's head.

17. Glue on buttons, beads, or other charms.

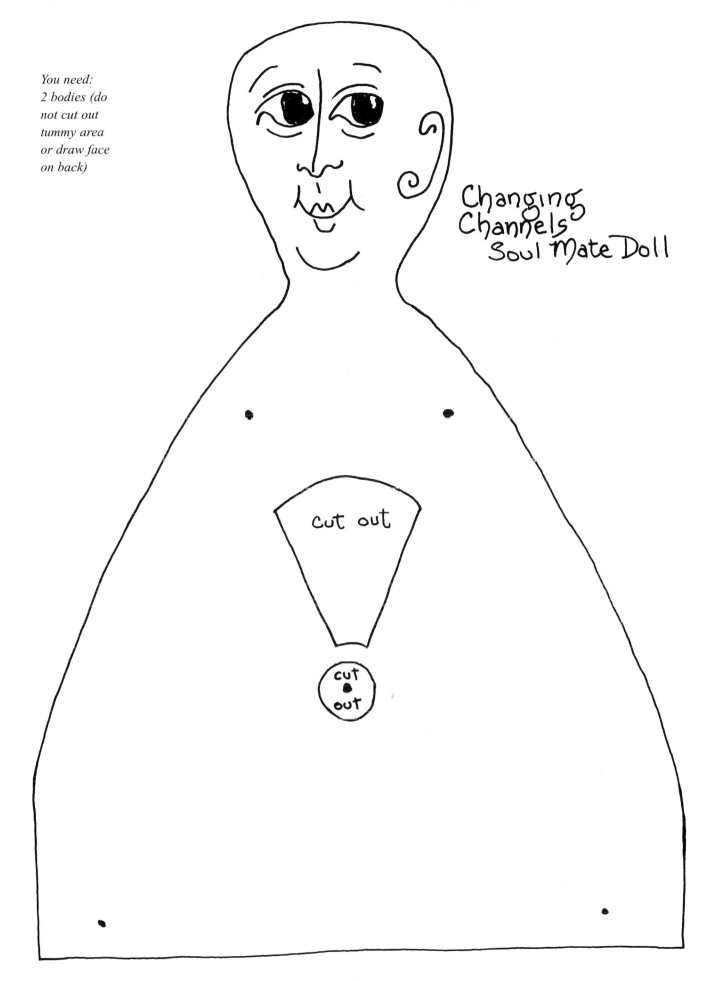

You need:
2 bodies (do
not cut out
tummy area
or draw face
on back)

Changing
Channels
Soul Mate Doll

cut out

cut
out

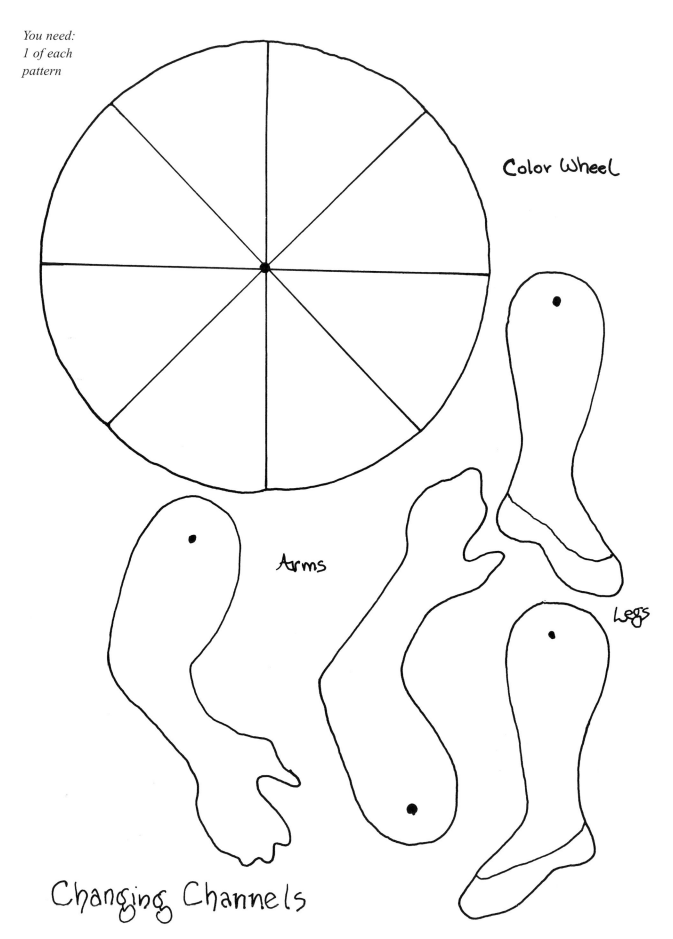

You need:
1 of each
pattern

Color Wheel

Arms

Legs

Changing Channels

Soul Mate Angel Doll for Courage

The Changing Channels Soul Mate Doll made me think about how life can sometimes force us to stretch our emotional muscles and act with courage. Summoning up images of angels helps me feel more courage, and that is why I designed this Angel Soul Mate Doll. She's made of one of my favorite materials: lace. Make her using the Flat Soul Mate Doll pattern (page 12).

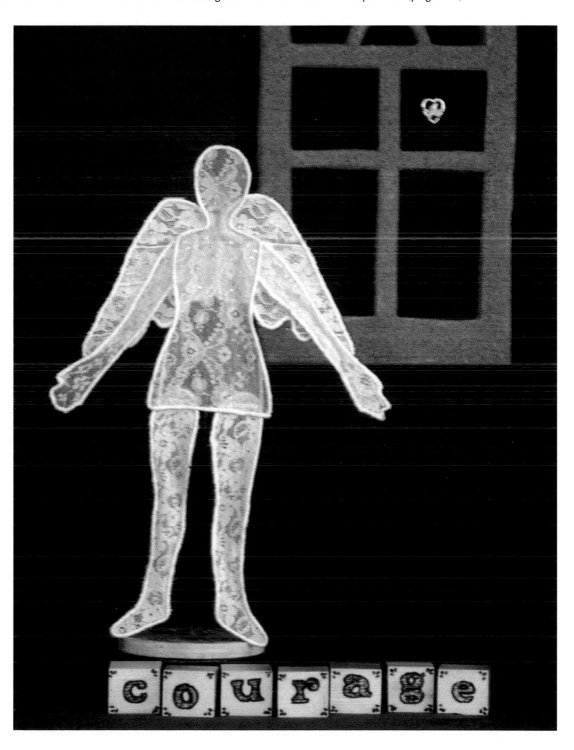

Materials and Tools

Safety glasses (**very important!**)
Spool of 18-gauge wire
Lace fabric or strips of lace zigzagged together
Optional: charms or buttons
Thread
Tracing paper
Sewing machine that does zigzag stitch
Extra sewing machine needle
Scissors
Vanishing ink marker
Wire cutters
Straight pins
Plastic 1" diameter curtain ring

1. Using the vanishing ink marker, trace the patterns onto tracing paper, leaving a small margin around each part. Trace the wing pattern onto tracing paper. Make sure to flip the arms and legs once, so that the hands and feet are in correct alignment. Paper-clip the upper arm to the lower arm to temporarily join them before tracing them. Draw two arms. Round off the tops of the legs when tracing them. Draw two legs and one body. Cut out the pattern pieces, leaving a fairly good margin of tracing paper around them.

2. Pin the tracing paper pieces on top of the lace. If your lace strips aren't wide enough, zigzag them together.

3. Prepare your sewing machine: If you can, drop the feed dogs out of action. Remove the presser foot or put on an embroidery foot. Lower the presser foot control to engage the thread tension. Set the stitch length to very short. Set the stitch width to medium.

4. **Note: Always wear safety glasses when working with this technique. You can break needles by hitting the wire with the needle, and bits can fly up in your face.** Unwind a few feet of wire from the spool or coil. Lay the wire on the outline of the pattern. Lower the needle into the lace/tracing paper combination slightly to one side of the line. As you sew, you will need to hold the wire in place in front of and behind the needle. Pushing down on the wire minimizes the wire's tendency to bounce around. Slowly sew along the line, encasing the wire in the zigzagging. The zigzag will form a satin stitch that will completely cover the wire. When you come to a turning point, lower the needle into the lace/tracing paper combination. Bend the wire per the shape of the piece

and continue sewing. Go very slowly to maintain control.

5. If you are using very fine wire, you may want to go around the outline of the doll a second time with the wire. This will make it sturdier. When you have sewn all around the piece, snip the wire about a 1/2" from the last bit of sewing. Slowly sew this piece of wire alongside the first bit of wire.

6. Carefully, with the sharp scissors, cut away any excess lace from the outside edges.

7. Pull away the tracing paper.

8. Set your zigzag to its widest width and sew around the outside edge again, capturing any frayed bits in the satin stitch.

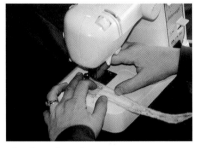

Circling the edge.

9. Repeat Steps 2-8 with all of the parts.

10. Joining: On the wrong side of the wings, zigzag the curtain ring in place just at the top of the "V" where the wings come together.

Trace the templates onto tracing paper and pin it to the lace.

Sewing the wire to the outline.

Sewing the ring to the wings.

With right sides up, place the legs under the body and stitch by zigzagging in place several times. Place the doll's body on the wings. Put the arms in place between the body and wings. Zigzag in place several times and snip the threads. Glue on optional charms or buttons.

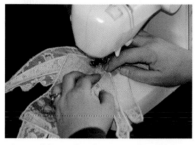

Assembling the Courage Soul Mate Doll.

Courage Soul Mate Doll Wing Pattern

You'll lay the wire along the outline & zig zag it to the lace

Anger and rage are two emotions that do not summon up the urge to make a Soul Mate Doll in me. Nope. When I get furious, I need intense physical action. Constructive things like weight lifting or charging up and down the stairs are good. Equally satisfying are controlled destruction actions that won't hurt me or anyone or anything. Well, anything important… Smashing a tacky ornament or a non-recyclable bottle can be deeply satisfying. Even the sweeping up afterwards is satisfying. The trash bin lid shutting down on it all seems to sigh, "Yup."

Ah, but resentment, now that's a different matter. That's one you can unravel slowly and examine. It's right in there, feeding envy and greed. Ugh.

I was feeling quite resentful one day, so I decided to make a portrait of the feeling. When I tried to think of what resentment would look like, it seemed to be all pulled in, pulled down, and very narrow. There was nothing expansive or open in the feeling. When I thought about what color it would be, it was *very* gray to me. So, that's the color I chose to go with. (No rosy cheeks for her!)

How would resentment move? Well, I couldn't imagine much flexibility, so I didn't want many joints. I saw her as being rigid and unbending, so only the arms are bent. Oh, and there *had* to be a pointing finger to lay some blame around, too. I was sure that there would be a tapping foot, so I drew upon the cartoon convention of "multiple imaging" it.

I tried putting spiky hair on her, but she didn't approve. She resented it! She wanted it *tight* and pulled back hard and slick.

When I thought about working on her back, she snapped, "Don't you dare go behind my back!" So I didn't.

I had a lot of fun making her, which turned around my horrible mood. Making her was the antidote to being stuck in a state of resentment. Looking at her cracks me up. Often, when I show her to people, they laugh as well, saying that, yes, they recognize that feeling, too.

Resentment Soul Mate Doll

The Resentment Doll is made with the Basic Flat Doll technique (page 11). Note that her right arm is joined to the back side of the body and the left arm is on the front. Make an extra joint at her wrists.

Materials and Tools

Gray paper*
Card stock (because this doll
  is fairly small, lightweight
  card stock works fine)
Paper clips or wire
Sharp craft knife
Cutting mat
Scissors
Glue
Hot glue gun and sticks
Wire snips
Needlenose pliers

*If you are using gray card stock,
copy the pattern directly onto the
card stock.

1. Copy pattern onto gray
paper and glue it to the card
stock.
2. Glue gray paper to the other
side of the card stock. Let dry.
3. Cut out doll parts.
4. Refer to page 13 for joint-
making directions.
5. Note that the left arm is on
top of the body section and the
right arm is under it.
6. Make joints for the wrists.

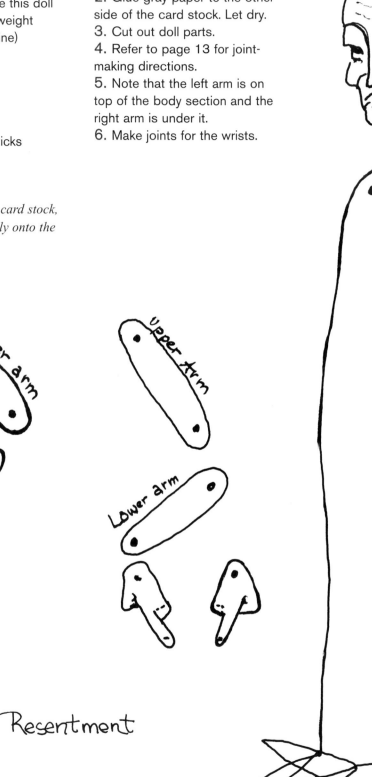

You need:
1 of each
pattern

Resentment

Thank You/Gratitude Soul Mate Doll

This may seem to be a peculiar pairing of Soul Mate Dolls, but I believe that gratitude is an excellent way to dislodge resentment. Do you have a hard time saying a simple "thank you" to a compliment? Isn't it odd how a compliment can bring up a rush of feeling, "Omigosh! I don't deserve that! Just think of all of the twerpy things I've ever done!" The bigger the compliment, the harder it can be to let it in. I think that a lot of people have this response. It can be hard to just say "thank you" to kind words.

The other meaning of this Soul Mate Doll is as an expression of gratitude for all of the blessings, beauty, wonder, and abundance that life has to offer. That's why I believe this is an important Soul Mate Doll to make.

I learned how to make "tassel" dolls when I was very young. I always called them "yarn dollies." I have no idea who taught me how to make them, but I am so grateful to whomever it was, because I have had enormous pleasure from them all of my life. First, I'll show you how to make "tassel" or "yarn" dolls and then how I have evolved Soul Mate Dolls from this technique. You can use all kinds of natural materials for the dolls' torsos or heads. If you find something that would work for the head, glue the tassel to the "neck" of the object and make the tassel into the body. You might find something, like a large pine cone, seashell, stone, or whatever, that would work for the torso. In that case, glue tassel arms and a tassel skirt to it. You might want to use the patterns for the head in the book, or you might choose to go with something else.

Materials and Tools

Hat: Set up the Lacis Square Loom to weave a 3" square, or a pin board loom set up to weave a 3" square. (See directions for setting up a 3" pin board loom on page 44.)

Note: If you don't want to weave a square for her hat, you can use a 3" square of fabric, paper, or felt in a shade that matches the doll's body.

1 ball worsted weight "dish-cloth" yarn (approx. 2 oz.)*
2 white 12" chenille stems
2 blue 12" chenille stems
4" by 8" of closely-woven fabric

Heart button or charm
Darning needle
Scissors
Hot glue gun and sticks
Permanent black fine-point marker
Tracing paper
Stuffing
Needle and thread
Book to wrap yarn around (I used my journal**; it is 9-3/4" by 7-3/4" by 1".)

Materials and Tools for Jig:

Small scrap of 3/4" plywood (4" square will do)
12 small finishing nails

(brads), each less than 1" long
Hammer

Note: You can also use a 4" square of sturdy foam or ceiling tile and twelve pins for a less permanent jig.

*Used in this project: * Lily Sugar 'n Cream cotton, #203, Blue Shadow; **Journal available from Lee Valley.*

1. Weave a 3" square for the hat or use a square of fabric, paper, or felt. (The remaining yarn will be used to make the body.)
2. Make the hands: Trace the pattern onto tracing paper and put on the board. Push in a pin

Basic Tassel or Yarn Doll

Materials and Tools

*Audio cassette case
Yarn* or thread (the finer the yarn, the smaller you can make the doll; just wrap it around a smaller object; use a larger object for thick yarn)*

**I used Lily Sugar 'n Cream cotton in #70, Lime to make this doll. One ball makes several dolls.*

1. *Wrap the yarn around the long side of an audio cassette case fifty times.*
2. *Slip it off the case, keeping your fingers inside of the loops to keep them organized. Cut a length of yarn and slip it inside the loops. Tie it in a knot at the top of the loops. This is the top of the head. Cut the ends.*
3. *Cut the lower edge of the loops open. Wrap a length of yarn around the neck several times and tie a knot tightly. (Use a square knot: left over right and under, right over left and under).*
4. *Separate out fifteen strands from each side for*

Left: Tassel Doll.

Right: Making a Tassel Doll.

the arms. Cut arms to length. Wrap yarn around wrists and knot. Wrap yarn around waist and knot. If you want, you can separate the strands for two legs, wrap around around ankles, and knot, or you can leave the skirt as is. Trim any untidy ends.

at each dot or hammer the nails into the wood, one nail to each dot. With a blue chenille stem, follow the numbered sequence, starting and ending at #1. Ease off jig. Squeeze the fingers together and shape a hand. Twist wrist shut. Repeat for the other hand.

The hat and hands for the Thank You Soul Mate Doll.

3. Face: Copy the pattern onto fabric with the permanent fine-point black marker. With right sides together, sew front to back. Cut out head, leaving a 1/4" seam allowance all around it. Pull the back away from the front and snip a 1" long opening, approximately 1" up from the lower edge. Turn head right side out.

4. Fold the two white chenille stems in half and insert the fold into the head. Holding the head face up, stuff it firmly. Be sure that the chenille stems lie at the back of the head, with the stuffing between them and the face. Stitch the fold of the chenille stems to the back of the top of the head.

5. The ends of the chenille stems are sticking out of the

head and will become the neck and backbone of the doll. Fold the fabric "back of head" section in half, right sides together. This makes a kind of cone shape. Stitch from dot to dot, leaving the center open. Turn right side out. Slip the back of the head section up the chenille stem neck, with the large end of the cone shape going up to the head. Turn under a 1/4" long seam allowance and stitch it to the head. Stitch the lower opening of the back of the head to the chenille stems. Twist the chenille stems for almost an inch to form the neck, then separate them into two pairs.

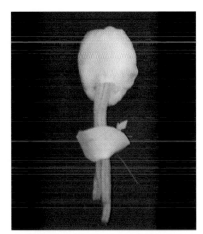

Making the back of the head for the Thank You Soul Mate Doll.

6. Wrap the yarn around the long edge of the journal or book. Slip the loops of yarn off the book, keeping your fingers inside of the loops to maintain order.

7. Cut the lower edge of the loops open. Lay the center of the strands up against the twisted neck section of the chenille stems. Twist the chenille stems, which will form her spine. Twist the chenille stems all the way to the ends. "Comb" the

strands down with your fingers and bury the chenille stems in the middle of the yard strands.

The chenille stems are locked around the yarn, which has been snipped off the journal.

8. Divide two arm sections of approximately thirty-five strands each away from body and lay them horizontal to the body. Cut any excess arm strands off. The arms should each measure about 4-1/2" from shoulder to wrist.

The arms have been cut.

9. Open the arm strands up slightly. Put a dab of hot glue on the wrist of the chenille stem hand. Place hand so that the ends of the yarn will come down

over the back of the hand, in a cuff. Wrap a short length of yarn around the wrist and glue in place. Repeat with the other hand.

The hands have been glued in.

10. Tie the waist. Wrap a couple of extra strands around and glue in place.

11. Optional: Wrap two strands of yarn around the neck and glue in place.

12. Separate the strands of yarn that were cut off the arms into groups of five to seven strands. Twist them tightly at the center. Fold in half and glue to the head for hair.

Wigging.

13. Glue the woven square to the head, with one point over the forehead.

14. Glue or sew the heart button to the chest.

15. If you want to make her a vest, the Skater's and Great Aunt Gardener's vests (pages 64 and 137, respectively) fit her well.

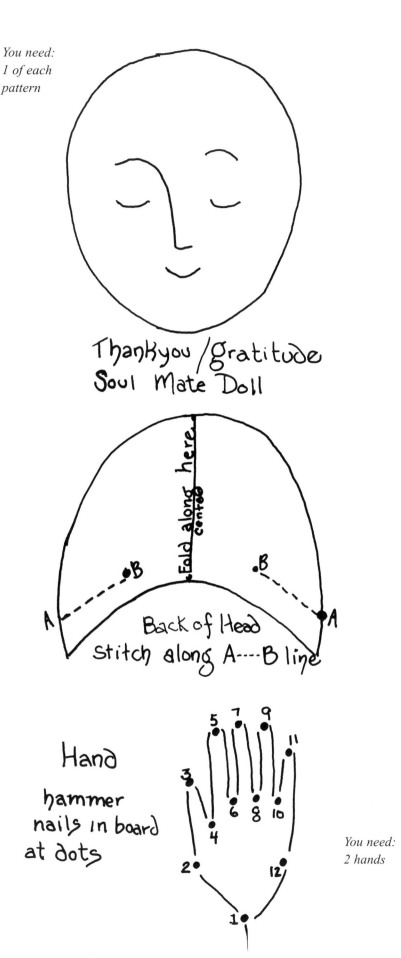

You need: 1 of each pattern

Thankyou /Gratitude Soul Mate Doll

Fold along here center

•B   •B

A ---   --- A

Back of Head
Stitch along A----B line

Hand

hammer nails in board at dots

You need: 2 hands

Grief Soul Mate Doll

When we have suffered a loss and are grieving, we still feel the presence of whom or what we loved and lost in our hearts. But our hands and arms are empty. Making a Soul Mate Doll gives us something to hold onto.

If you are grieving, please look through the book and see if one or more of the Soul Mate Dolls speaks to your feelings. What are you feeling? Is it loss, abandonment, emptiness, lethargy, anger, sorrow, or regret? See if there are Soul Mate Dolls that address those feelings, and then make them.

When my friend, Heather, died I made many, many of the Lace Angel Soul Mate Dolls (the Soul Mate Doll for Courage). Not long after Heather passed away, our dear cat, Sophie, died. What a sorrowful time it was. To help with my grieving, as well as making the Lace

Angels, I made tassel dolls with angel wings. Some of the tassel dolls were made with sticks, stones, bones, seashells, and other natural objects I found when on walks. These dolls, and the making of them, really helped with both losses. When I look at them now, I remember the beauty of these two special friends.

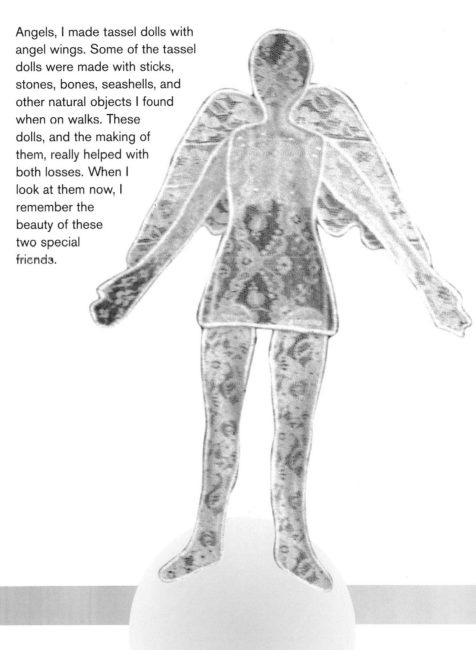

Cat Angel Soul Mate Doll

To make the Cat Angel Soul Mate Doll, follow the directions for the Thank You Doll (page 83), omitting the hat and hair. I used one ball (approx. 2 oz.) Lily Sugar'n Cream cotton #195, Tangerine Dream Variegated for her body. I painted her face with acrylics and colored pencil. To make her wings, I used the Lacis Square Loom set up for a 4" square. You can also weave a 4" square on a pin board loom (see page 24). Alternative wings can be made from lace, silk plant leaves, fabric, paper, or felt. Pleat the square on the diagonal, wrap yarn around the gathers, and glue it to the back of the body.

Making the wings for the Cat Angel Soul Mate Doll

You need:
1 pattern

Cat Angel Soul Mate Doll

Forgiveness Fairy Soul Mate Doll

Forgiveness is a fierce emotion, not in the least "namby pamby." It is a resolution to actively release and move forward. It's another important antidote to resentment.

Forgiveness Fairy Doll Visualization

Forgiving can be a difficult thing to do. This visualization and the Soul Mate Doll you will make from it might be useful to you if you have some forgiving to do. (Don't we all?)

First of all, get very comfortable. Turn off the phone, the radio, as much of the world as you can. Have the lights comfortably low. If there is a lot of outside noise, consider using earplugs. (You may wish to tape this.)

Close your eyes for a moment and breathe slowly and deeply, all of the way down to your toes. Feel the cool air gently bringing life into you. Take all you need from the air. Let it clean and replenish all of the molecules in your body. Let it go.

Now, imagine that a wise old woman has come to join you. She is wearing a long, full skirt that has many pockets and possibilities. She carries an ancient sewing basket that is closed, but full.

She says to you, "There's something I want to show you." She pulls a magic flashlight out of one of her pockets and says, "This light will show you something that you need to see more clearly." She shines the light on you, and you see, with a shock, that there is a hollow, flexible tube coming out of you. You see where it is attached to you, and you see that it is pulsing with energy that is draining out of you. She shines the light down the tube and you follow it— down, down, oh, no! It's attached to an unspeakably ugly little creature! The creature is small, but dense, heavy, and is everything that you know to be repulsive. Then you notice that it is feeding, greedily, voraciously, sucking the energy out of the tube—living off of your energy!

You are appalled and try to get away from it, but you can't. You try to stomp on it, but that only makes it stronger.

You turn to the old woman for help. "Speak to it," she says, "it is a feeling. Ask it to tell you what feeling it is and where it came from."

You turn back to the grotesque creature. "What feeling are you?" It swivels an oozing eye at you and croaks, "I am _____ (Rage, Hate, Loathing, Revenge, Destruction, Lethargy, Defeat, Collapse, Self Pity, Self Righteousness...)"

"Where did you come from?" you ask it.

"From the time that _____ did (or didn't) _____ to (for, with) you."

You recoil in shock, knowing that it is true.

The old woman says to you, "It's time to stop feeding this creature."

You agree. She reaches into a pocket and pulls out a very small, but strong clamp. You take the clamp from her, and wherever the tube enters your body, whether at your ankle, belly, shoulder, hip, jaw, wherever, you open the clamp and close it over the tube. Sensing your intention, the ugly creature snarls and flails at you, menacing you, threatening you. The old lady touches your hand and looks into your eyes, giving you strength. She waits with you, as the life pulse in the tube dims and goes out. The creature gasps and dies. The tube shrivels up and falls away from your body. The old lady puts on gloves and lifts a small wooden box out of her basket. She puts the body of the horror in the box and carries it to a fire. She places the box in the fire and it is totally consumed by the fire.

The clamp has fallen away from your body. She gives you a special ointment for the little wound the tube has left. It heals the wound completely, leaving not a mark. The old lady says to you, "I have something for you, my dear."

She places a seed in your hand. It is a curious seed, oddly shaped, larger than most. You are puzzled by it. She explains to you, "It is the Seed of Forgiveness. Let's plant it and see what grows."

Together you prepare a place for it. Because it is a magical seed, it can be planted in an unusual place, such as the moss on a stone, the base of a branch, or in the heart of a flower. Prepare the place and plant the seed. Sit back and watch as the seed begins to wake up. It rocks and splits the covering. A tentative tiny root reaches out, exploring. You feel a movement in your heart that matches the movement of the root. The root grows longer and stronger. The feeling of peace and contentment grows and deepens in your heart.

Next, a green shoot emerges, reaching, pulsing toward the light. You feel a sense of anticipation and delight as the tender little shoot lifts and unfurls itself. It gains strength and becomes vibrant and strong. A bud emerges at the tip, and before your eyes, a blossom fills, throbs into being. The blossom swings this way and that, seeking the light, filling the air with glorious scent.

It begins to open, and lo and behold! There is a tiny fairy at the heart of the flower. The little fairy has wings, delicate and new. This little being is quite wonderful, amazing, and different than any other you have ever seen or imagined. Notice the colors, the textures, the shapes. You gently reach out and caress it, loving it. It responds to your tender touch with delight. It hops up into your hand and gestures to you that it wants to speak to you. You lift it to your ear and it whispers a message. You listen deeply to its message.

Spend as much time as you wish with this wonderful little one. When you ask its name, it joyfully announces, "Call me Forgiveness!"

The two of you have fun together, while the old lady quietly looks on. Then you know it is time for Forgiveness to take flight.

You lift your hands high, and perching on your fingertips, Forgiveness leaps up and soars. You watch the flight, and your heart soars, too.

Forgiveness calls to you, "I will always be with you, whenever you need me, I will be with you!"

You and the old woman laugh

at the antics of Forgiveness in flight, the loops and midair twirls, the fun, and the sheer joy. The old lady points to the ground and you see not gray shadows where Forgiveness passes, but rainbows, rainbows everywhere.

When you are ready, you come back to this time and place.

Get your notebook out and write or draw all that you can remember about the Forgiveness Fairy.

Now, it's time to make a Soul Mate Doll of Forgiveness, so that every time you look at the doll, even if you don't consciously realize it, her message of joy and release will deepen in your heart and mind.

Ask yourself: How big should I make my Forgiveness Fairy? What colors? What textures? Should I make a flat doll, or should I use another technique? Remember that you can make endless numbers of Forgiveness Fairy Soul Mate Dolls, so that every aspect and element of forgiveness doesn't have to be in just one. Also remember that Forgiveness is a magical being able to change shape and form constantly, so you don't have to be "perfect" about how you represent it each time, because it is the feeling tone that is key. Here are instructions for one particular version.

Making the Forgiveness Fairy

There are pocket dolls, and there are pocket dolls...

Sometimes it's important to have a Soul Mate Doll that is able to contain messages and little objects. The doll needs to have a pocket or pouch as a major component to hold onto precious things—things that help us remember, release, to be more who we are truly meant to be. The pocket part of the Forgiveness Fairy Soul Mate Doll helps us make our insights and revelations more real. It gives us a "keeping place" for notes and the other small physical objects that are the symbols of the newly-acquired wisdom.

Materials and Tools

Worsted weight "dishcloth" yarn or wool (approx. 1 oz.)*
Charms** or buttons
1" diameter button
2" diameter circle of closely-woven skin-tone fabric
Lacis Square Loom set up to weave 2" squares, pin board loom***, or a 2" Weavette Loom
Note: If you don't want to weave the squares, you can use 2" squares of felt or fleece.
Needle and thread
Darning needle
Scissors
Small snap closer
Craft stick
Hot glue gun and sticks
Small clamp
Pinch of stuffing
Permanent black fine-point marker

*Used in this project: *Bernat Berella Muskoka Merino wool, worsted, aran weight in #9848, Rose Arbour; **"Hearts III" charms from Birdhouse Enterprises.*

***For the pin board loom, you will need a 4" piece of sturdy pink or blue foam insulation board, at least 1" thick, or a ceiling tile that's been wrapped with plastic wrap and taped to lessen the dust coming off it. You will also need a 4" piece of 1/4" graph paper and eighteen pins. Place this paper to the board. Insert nine pins every 1/4" along the line, 1" from the lower edge and 1" from the side. Insert nine pins every 1/4" along the line, 1" from the upper edge and 1" from the side.*

1. Weave four 2" square squares. If you don't want to weave the squares, you can use four 2" square squares of felt or fleece. The squares are used to make the front and back of the pouch that form the body, the square that closes the pouch while forming the shoulders, and the wings.

2. Baste around the edges of the fabric circle. Place the bit of stuffing on its center and then put the button on that. Draw up basting stitches tightly. On the front of this covered button, draw a face with the permanent black fine-point marker.

Making the face for the Forgiveness Fairy.

3. Make two twisted cords, following the directions in the sidebar on page 45. These will be for the arms and legs. They

will use four 24" long strands of yarn. Tie knots at both ends to make the hands and feet.

4. Fold the leg cord in half. Place one square on top of another. Sew down one side. Place the center fold of the leg cord inside the lower edge, with the legs hanging out. Sew along the lower edge, catching in the fold. Sew the third side. Weave in any loose ends. This forms the pouch, which is the doll's body.

Making the face for the Forgiveness Fairy.

5. Cut the craft stick in half. Glue the wrong side of the face button to the cut end. Fold a woven square in half diagonally. This square will be the doll's shoulders. Push the round end

Glue the craft stick inside the pouch, to the back square.

of the craft stick through the center. Slide the diagonal square right up to the head. Leaving the shoulder square free, glue the wrong side of the craft stick to the inside of the back square of the "body pouch," making sure it is centered.

6. Glue the back point of the shoulder square to the outside of the body back. Glue the center of the arm cord to the front of the craft stick, inside the doll, where the shoulder square folds over.

Glue in the arms.

7. Wings: Weave in the loose ends. Pull two corners of the square to elongate it (also do this if you are using felt). Squeeze the square at the center, pleating it. Wrap the center tightly with yarn a few times and knot it. Pull the wings

Glue on the wings.

into a pleasing shape and glue to the doll's upper back.

8. Hair: Make a twisted cord with four 36" lengths of yarn (see page 45). Glue the loops to the outside edge of the face.

Glue on the hair.

9. Sew the small snap fastener inside the lower front point of the shoulder square and to the body front. Glue or sew the heart charms onto the doll.

10. Place notes, poems, dreams, or other remembrances inside doll.

Forgiveness Fairy Face

Yes! and No! Soul Mate Dolls

I made the Yes! Soul Mate Doll in response to an exceptionally "Yes" experience. Several people said, after revealing the "Yes" beneath the heart, "This should say "No!"

"Why?"

"Because I don't know how to say it!" Oh, oh.

I hope these Yes! and No! Soul Mate Dolls help. They are made with a variation on the Flat Soul Mate Doll technique (page 11).

Materials and Tools

Sturdy non-corrugated card stock
Paper
Chenille stems, yarn, baler twine, or packing cord
Trims such as ribbon or lace, buttons, charms, etc.
Paper clips
Paints and paintbrushes, colored pencils, or crayons
Glue
Sharp craft knife and cutting mat
Scissors
Needlenose pliers
Hot glue gun and sticks
Wire cutters
Pencils and eraser
Vanishing ink marker
Carbon paper
Awl or darning needle
A couple of clamps

1. Copy the front, flip it over, and trace it onto another sheet of card stock to make a back. Make two arms and one heart for each doll. Glue to sturdy non-corrugated card stock.

2. Cut out the circle in the front.

3. On the doll front, make holes at the shoulder and below the circle and in the base of the heart.

4. With the vanishing ink marker or pencil, trace the circle twice onto white paper.

5. With a permanent marker, write "Yes!" or "No!," being sure to fit the word inside the circle.

6. Cut out the Yes or No circles, leaving at least a 1/2" around the outline. Center the word in the circle on the inside of the front sections, then glue it in place.

"Yes" is glued inside the circle.

7. Paint on the shoes and stockings.

8. Paint the dress.

9. Paint the doll's face, using either the one provided or one you have drawn.

10. Paint the arms. Place the arm on a piece of cardboard and press down with either the awl or darning needle and turn it to make holes.

11. Straighten and cut a paper clip into three equal pieces. With your needlenose pliers, make a small loop at one end.

Push the end through the right side of the heart and then through the hole at the base of the tummy hole, so that the loop is holding the heart to the tummy.

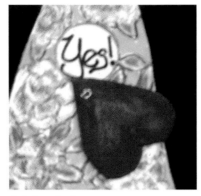

Joining the heart.

On the wrong side of doll front, twist the wire into a loop, right down to the body. Fold over the loops so that they hold the heart snugly to the body. Squeeze them tightly so they are firmly in place.

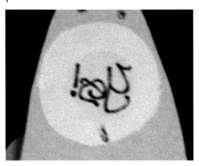

The back side of the front.

12. Make two more wire loops for the arms. The loop end is on the outside of the body front.

Joining the arms.

Put the arms on the inside of the body. Close the loop on the arm so that it moves snugly.

13. Spread a smooth layer of glue on the inside of the head, lower half of dress, legs, and feet (the wrong side of the doll's front).

14. Clamp the body back to the front.

15. Add whatever kind of hair you like, in whatever style appealing to you. I used chenille stems, wrapped around a ruler and pencil for "No," cut the chenille stems into 3" lengths for "Yes," and hot-glued them to their heads.

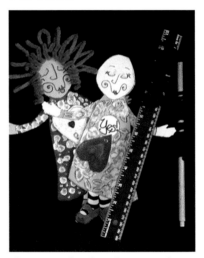

One way of making hair is with chenille stems.

16. Instead or Yes or No, you could put any message your heart desires in the circle. One possibility is to make a special Remembrance Soul Mate Doll, with a name, date, or message in the circle.

Yes! and No!

Soul Mate Dolls

To make the back turn the front over & trace the outline.

You need:
2 bodies
1 of each
remaining
pattern

back of shoes

Recovery Soul Mate Doll

The other morning the sun came out after what felt like weeks of gray weather. Suddenly, I felt myself filling up with life and energy. I thought, "Ah, the sun renews and restores me!" This thought set off a chain of word connections, all of them "R" words that had to do with healing: resolving, reclaiming, restoring, releasing, re-creating, recognizing, reshaping, reframing, recovery, recovering, recovered, reweaving the web of life. And so I was inspired to design Recovery Soul Mate Dolls.

Above: Recovery Soul Mate Dolls.
Right: The backs of the Recovery Soul Mate Dolls.

We all have suffered losses of one sort or another, whether physical, emotional, intellectual, or spiritual. But I do believe that there is something encoded in our genes that wants to lead us back to wellness. I call that the Imprint of Wholeness. It is like a gyroscope that insistently urges us to find a point of balance, even in the midst of the most enormous chaos.

As I thought about what a Recovery Soul Mate Doll would look like, I realized that there could never be just one way of making her. The metaphor of weaving is really powerful for me, so I wanted to weave at least one. I traced the Basic Flat Soul Mate Doll template onto 1/4" graph paper and set up a pin

board loom. Insert pins at each of the numbered points and follow the numbered sequence to warp the doll pieces. Note that you can weave any shape piece by using this technique.

Materials and Tools

Yarn or floss* (you can use a different color for each body piece)

Optional: charms**, buttons, or other trims

Sturdy foam insulation board or ceiling tile

Pins

Scissors

Darning needle

Stuffing

Optional: small narrow ruler or short knitting needle

*Used in this project: *Bernat Handicrafter crochet cotton, #10, Ecru for the warp; Muskoka 9838 Denims and 9848 Rose Arbour for the body; Bernat Cot'n Soft: 10916 Teal, 11381 Orange, 10924 Purple, 11379 Lime, 10919 Ligonberry; Lily Sugar'n Cream: 38 Persimmon, 95 Red, 16 Dark Pine for the arms and legs; in the photos, I used three skeins each of Caron Watercolours in Royal Jewels and Charcoal (warped with Lily Sugar'n Cream Black); **"Mini Hearts" charms from Birdhouse Enterprises.*

Note that you will weave two body, four arm, and four leg pieces.

Important: Never pull out the lower line of pins until you are completely finished weaving that piece.

1. Copy the pin board pattern and place it on the foam board. Insert pins at a 30-degree angle away from the outline of the piece. The lettered sides of the head are warped after the numbered sequence has been followed, cut, and knotted. Retie the warp at "A," warp to "E" in sequence, cut, and knot. Repeat from "F" to "J."

The pin board loom is warped, and the various parts of a woven Recovery Doll are laid out.

2. Begin at the lower straight edge and work a row of Soumak stitch (see page 24). I wove under one warp, then over, under two warps across to the last warp, and over the last one. When weaving the body, pull in the weft to form the waist and spread it again and pin at the sides for the chest. Shape the wrist, knee, and ankles the same way.

3. As you weave up to and past the shoulders, you can remove pins #2, 26, 4, 24, 6, 22, 8, 20, 10, and 18 one at a time as you go through the loop of warp on those pins. Never pull out the lower pins until the entire piece is woven.

4. When you reach the loose ends of warp that are hanging off the lettered pins, tie a square knot to the weft with the ends.

5. To shape the hands, after you weave up to the wrist, move pins #6 and 8 at least 1/4" to the right.

Move pin #2 1/4" to the left.

6. Sewing the front and back pieces together: Holding the wrong sides together, go down through a couple of weft threads at the edge of the front piece, then down through a couple of weft threads at the edge of the back piece. Repeat. (It's a slight variation on the Baseball stitch, page 25.)

7. Sew the edges of the head together first, stuff it, and then sew the rest of the body together, leaving the lower edge open for stuffing. Stuff and then sew it shut.

8. When sewing the fronts and backs of the arms and legs together, start at the corner of the lower edge, sew up one side seam, and around the hand or foot. Stuff the hand or foot, sew a little further, and stuff. Continue until the arm or leg is completely sewn together and stuffed.

9. Sew the arms and legs to the body. Sew or glue charms to the body.

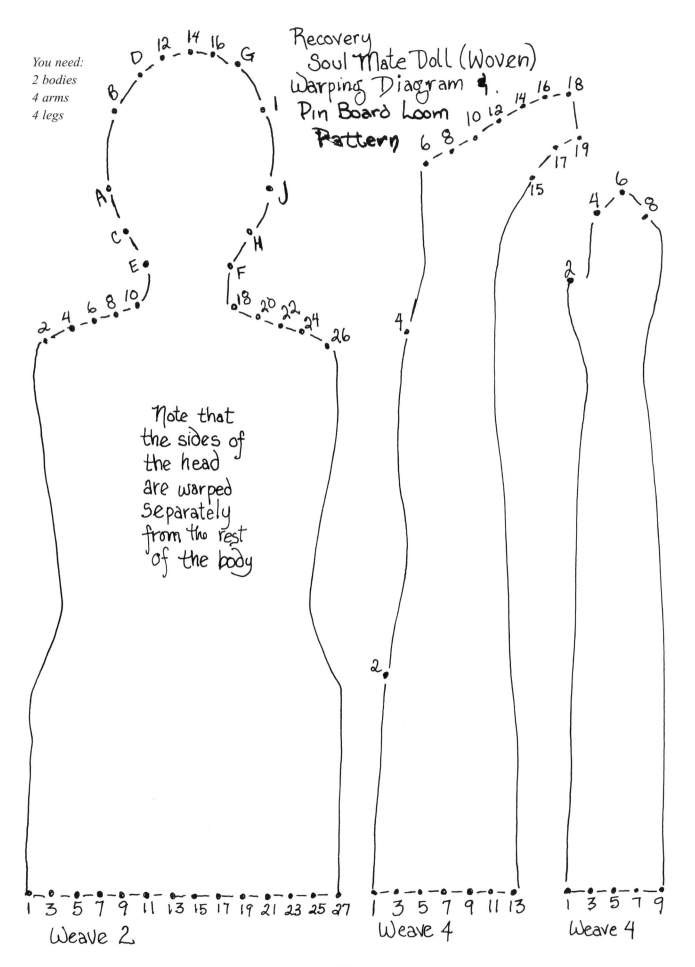

You need:
2 bodies
4 arms
4 legs

Recovery
Soul Mate Doll (Woven)
Warping Diagram 4.
Pin Board Loom
Pattern

Note that
the sides of
the head
are warped
separately
from the rest
of the body

Weave 2

Weave 4

Weave 4

Painted Recovery Soul Mate Doll

I also wanted to do a painted Recovery Soul Mate Doll that was three-dimensional, so I used the Basic Flat Soul Mate Doll templates (page 12) to make a sewn and stuffed version. I painted her after she was stuffed and omitted the hair. Follow the instructions for the Serenity Doll on page 21 to make one for yourself.

If neither of these Soul Mate Dolls feels right to you, perhaps start by making yourself a Basic Flat Soul Mate Doll. Allow yourself to break some rules about what a doll should look like and what a doll should be made from.

Another approach to the Recovery Soul Mate Doll might be to find a way of representing in the doll whatever is paining you. (This is a good time to use the Coloring Pages technique.) Then imagine what a Soul Mate Doll would look like with that pain healed and make that version.

Set the image of the pain an appropriate distance away from the "healed" Soul Mate Doll and imagine what it would take to bring them together. Perhaps this will help you visualize the next step on your healing path.

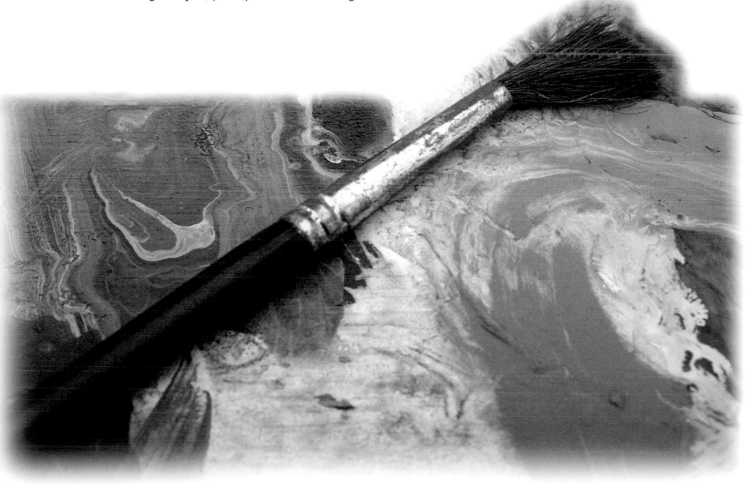

5chapter

The Playful Heart

When we have a playful heart, we are able to look at the world with clarity, vigor, and delight. We can make great leaps of creativity and unexpected connections. Laughter is one of the best side effects of having a playful heart.

First things first. You need to give yourself permission to take the risks you need to so you can cultivate a playful heart. A playful heart is the perfect antidote to the culture of cynicism that pervades us. A cynical heart lives in darkness, mistrusting everyone and everything. It scorns, lashes out at, and mocks that which it does not trust. It is destructive and leads to stagnation. It is unable to learn.

How can one take risks and grow in the face of attitudes like that? Protect yourself as much as you can from the sneering cynics, and for heaven's sake, don't become one yourself!

Flexibility is one of the keys to having a playful heart. It means being willing to try a new way of seeing the world. It's as if the old way of being has been outgrown, like an old coat–just like this visualization:

The Stumbling Block Coat

Make your space quiet and get comfortable. Breathe deeply, relaxing your neck and stomach muscles and jaw. Breathe in and out, wiggling your toes in anticipation. (You may wish to tape this.)

The Stumbling Block Coat (and variations).

Stumbling Block Visualization

Now, imagine a path at your feet. You start to walk along it. As you walk, you notice that you are not moving easily or gracefully. You become aware that you keep tripping over the hem of a long, clumsy coat. This is not a comfortable coat. It has sharp, picky things caught in it that snag your skin and scratch you. It is heavy, itchy, and flaps around your legs, causing you to stumble. The armholes are too small, so it binds and pulls across your back and under your arms. Why on earth would anyone wear such a dreadful coat?

Then you notice that it is made up of squares or blocks, and each one has something written on it. You are shocked to recognize your own handwriting! You are the one who has made this Stumbling Block Coat! The blocks say: "I can't _____," "You always _____," "I should _____," "You never _____," and more, so many more…

You sit down, feeling over-whelmed by the Stumbling Block Coat, ready to give up. All of a sudden, you hear a deep, rhythmic humming. The biggest, fuzziest, most charming bumble bee you have ever seen lifts her head from the depths of a flower beside you. She gazes at you with ancient, huge, wise eyes that have a twinkle of humor.

She says to you, "Well, you've gotten yourself into a fine state!"

You are startled by her speaking to you.

"Don't be silly," she buzzes, "anything can happen here! Now, come along. You need a friend. Dance with me."

She lifts up into the air and begins a stately dance that you do your best to follow. It is hard because of the Stumbling Block Coat, but certainly not as hard as before. In fact, the more you dance along behind the bee, the easier it becomes. She leads you to a lovely garden and tells you to come in.

A man is working, raking the ground around a fire pit. He is quietly, happily working while his two young children are playing.

The bee insists that you move forward, but you feel shy, an intruder in this peaceful scene. She buzzes over to the man and says, "I see you have a fine blaze going there—good, we need it!"

She asks you, "Are you ready to get rid of your Stumbling Block Coat?"

You think, "Am I ready? Am I willing to give up all of these stumbling blocks? I know this coat so well! What will I wear instead?"

You decide whether or not you are willing to give up the Stumbling Block Coat. When you are, you struggle with it, to get free of it. The man and bee see your difficulty and offer to help. You accept their help, and it becomes easier. The children see you twisting and turning, working yourself free of it, and they run over, delighting in this new game. They pull at the hem, and suddenly, you shoot out of the coat. Free! But cold.

You take the coat and push it into the fire. The fire blazes up, shooting sparks like fireworks. The children dance excitedly in the shower of sparks, so many colors, so much light! "Play for us, daddy!" The man laughs and pulls a small flute from his pocket and plays. You join in the dance.

Hearing the laughter and music, a woman comes out of the house. You realize that you have been hearing a muffled thumping sound and that when she joined you, the sound has stopped. She is a weaver, and her arms are full of exquisitely colored fabric.

She smiles at you and says, "I am so glad that you finally gave that hideous old thing up! I've been working on this for you, but I couldn't finish it until you let go of that ugly old Stumbling Block Coat! Now, try this on for size." She unfurls the most beautiful coat you have ever seen in your life—such colors! And the patterns! Never have you seen such glory before! It shimmers and shifts and you are overcome by its beauty.

"Come on, you're freezing! Try it on—I made it just for you!"

You slip into it, and indeed, it is made just for you. Such elegant comfort! You twirl and swirl and throw your arms around the weaver in thanks, laughing and crying.

"It is a Coat of All Possibilities," she says, "remember to wear this coat on your journey. It will lighten your load and ease the path, nurturing and inspiring you." You feel light and filled with grace.

You slip your hand into one of the pockets and feel something: a small doll. The weaver smiles at you and says, "This is the Doll of All Possibilities. She is for you." You thank her for her gifts and the bee for leading you to this enchanted place. You say goodbye to the children and their father, and in your own time and in your own way, you come back to your own space.

Coat Pattern for Flat Soul Mate Dolls

This pattern can be used to make a Stumbling Block Coat. By copying the pattern exactly as it is, it will fit any standard-size Flat Doll made from the patterns on page 12. This is an homage to traditional "Tumbling Block" quilt patterns.

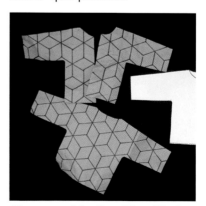

The parts of the Stumbling Block Coat.

I made the Stumbling Block Coat out of brown paper that I colored and then distressed by scrunching it up, over and over. The paper coat does not use any seam allowances (whereas a sewn coat needs to have 1/4" seam allowances added). I turned in an edge at the center and sewed small buttons on. I drew, but did not cut open, the buttonholes.

To make it, cut a template for the coat. Cut two front sections and one back by placing the template on the fold at center back.

Embellish and color it, glue it together at the seams, and hang it up. I sewed "Bee and Butterfly" charms from Birdhouse Enterprises to the coat.

To make a hanger, you need a real one out of your closet, needlenose pliers, and some soft wire. Measuring against your doll coat, follow the same "flight plan" as the real hanger. Add some curlicues to make it really your own.

Use the outline for the coat to make one or more Coat of All Possibilities. Feel free to make the coat in materials you might never have thought of before. Gather up things you find in nature and see how you can include them in a Coat of All Possibilities.

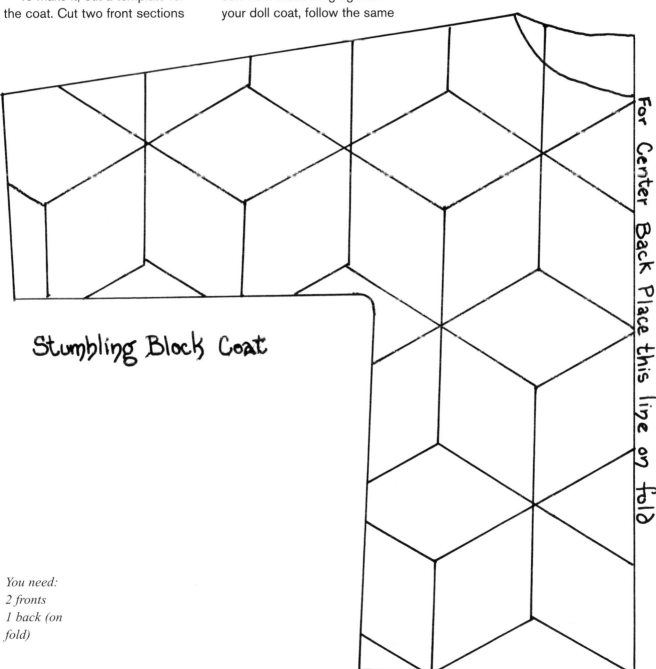

Stumbling Block Coat

For Center Back Place this line on fold

You need:
2 fronts
1 back (on fold)

The Doll of All Possibilities, the Seed Child Soul Mate Doll

The Doll of All Possibilities is a Seed Child Soul Mate Doll which symbolizes the planting, and replanting, of the seeds of creativity; it represents the potential for growth and new life.

If you are at a crossroads in your life, it can be good to name each part of the journey that has brought you to this crossroads. Name where you've been and where you're going. Fold this into the Seed Child Soul Mate Doll and see how you can make the new life blossom.

Materials and Tools

Scarf or handkerchief, approximately 12" to 16" square (If you use fabric instead of a hanky, hem the edges with a very narrow rolled (not serged) edge. It's fine to use lace trim around the edge.)
Wad of cotton batting or polyester stuffing
White thread
Small brass safety pin (or a significant pin)

1. Take the batting and hold the handkerchief over it, approximately 4" from one corner. Wrap thread around the handkerchief, tying the batting into a ball. Knot and then cut the thread. This is the doll's head.

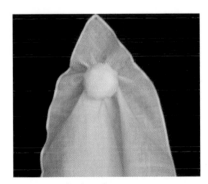

Forming the head.

2. Lay the hanky wrong side up on a table (with the doll's head not visible for the moment). Bring the two side corners toward the middle. Fold one corner over the other.

Flip it over and fold the corners back.

3. Bring the lower point up to, and slightly past, the point above the doll's head.

Fold up the bottom point.

4. Turn the doll over. Arrange the excess hanky gathered up around the head so it forms a cap around the face. Fold the "extra bits" down to tidy it up. Fold the side edges into the center, forming a triangle.

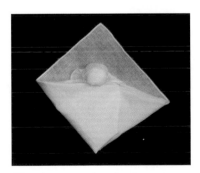

Turn it over and make the cap.

5. Bring the point of the triangle up and fold the point in so that it is tucked in under the chin.

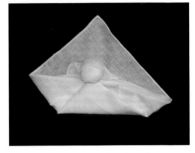

Tuck the point under the chin.

6. Fold the sides to the middle, overlapping them, and turning the upper edges outward. Pin in place.

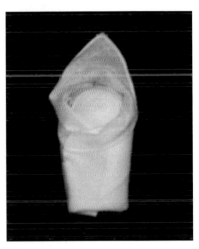

Fold the sides in and pin in place.

Magical Children Soul Mate Dolls

The children in the visualization are Magical Children. I hope that these little Soul Mate Dolls will remind you of the power of the playful heart. They are made in the Basic Flat Soul Mate Doll technique (page 11).

The knitted sweater is made using the pattern on page 15. I worked it with 1.5mm needles, using Wildflowers by Caron, Nefertiti. I made the crocheted sweater using the pattern on page 15 and a 1.5mm crochet hook and Wildflowers by Caron, Passion.

Materials and Tools

Card stock (I used card stock
   that is white on one side)
Optional: white paper
4" length of 1-1/2" to 2" wide
   ribbon
Glue
Scissors
Paint and paintbrush

1. Copy and glue the patterns
to card stock. Glue plain paper
to the back of the card stock

(optional). When the glue is dry,
cut out all of the parts.
2. Paint the T-shirt.
3. Draw hair lines and add
color. Color a little pinkish blush
on the cheeks.
4. Join arms and legs.
5. Shorts: Gather one long
edge of the ribbon. Pull up the
gathering thread and tie around
waist. Leave an opening at the
back. Either glue or sew the
center back seam. Pull the
inseam back between the legs
and glue or stitch in place.

*Making the shorts for the Magical
Children.*

magical Children
soul mate Dolls

*You need:
1 of each
pattern*

Mermaid Soul Mate Doll

When I was a little girl, it would take hours to walk to and from school, which I loathed. I would pretend to be a mermaid, and had incredible adventures which took a very long time to unfold. To me, mermaids are the essence of the playful heart.

Here's a pattern for a woven mermaid's tail. You will use it to make a tail-shaped pin board loom. If you don't want to weave it, you can use the outline to make a cloth of paper tail. Trace around the outline of the tail for a paper or felt tail and glue the edges of the tail together. If you would like to make it from fabric, add a 1/4" seam allowance and

sew it, right sides together, then turn right side out. You will need to clip the curved edges.

Materials and Tools for Tail

Yarn (approx. 2 oz.)*
Pin board loom: 8-1/2" by 11" of 1" to 2" thick blue or pink dense foam insulation (or

dense acoustical tile or similar board covered with plastic wrap and taped)
Pins
Scissors
Darning needle
Small clamp
Optional: small knitting needle or narrow ruler
Optional: paint or felt-tip marker

*Used in this project: *I usually use the same yarn for the warp and weft, but for the Mermaid's tail, I used crochet cotton for the warp and "dishcloth" weight cotton for the weft. This is completely optional, so feel free to use the same yarn for both. I used Bernat Handicrafter Crochet Cotton, #10, Ecru for the warp, and Lily Sugar'n Cream #202 Midnight Magic for the weft.*

Materials and Tools for Upper Body

Use the materials and tools listed for the Basic Flat Soul Mate Doll (page 9)

1. Using the Basic Flat Soul Mate Doll templates (page 12), make a body and arms, but no legs. Paint the face. Trim her hips in order to slip her body into the tail after it is woven.

2. Copy the pattern, lay it on your backing board, and insert pins at a 30-degree angle. They point out and away from the body of the weaving. Weave two tails (front and back). Use the same pattern for both.

3. Note that the body is warped in three sections: A, the right fin; B, the main part of the tail; and C, the left fin. Tie the warp cotton to pin #1 of the B, or main tail, section. Be *very* careful to follow the numbers—this is crucial. Warp from pins #1 to 37. Cut yarn and tie off. Rejoin warp at #1A, warp from pins #1A to 17A, cut warp, and tie off. Rejoin warp at pin #1C and warp from pins #1C to 17C.

The pin board loom for the Mermaid's tail.

4. Start weaving at pin #37 of the main tail. You will start a row by going under, over, and across, ending up with an "over." Repeat for another row. It is very important to "capture" the warp threads with the weft; otherwise, it will all unravel. (This is why you wove under one, over one for the first two rows.) Now, continue weaving the tail by going over two, under two.

5. As you weave up the tail, and come to pins #2, 36, 4, 34, 6, 32, 8, and 30, insert the darning needle into the loop of warp and weave across the row. You will need to repeat this in both the upper and lower edges of the fins.

6. When you weave up to 1A and 1C, tie the warp end with a square knot to the weft (right over left and under, left over right and under).

7. When you are weaving the fins, there are times when you'll have to weave single warps until you get up to a point where you can "double up" again.

8. When you reach the two center pins, #18 and 20, you will weave the rest of each fin separately.

9. When weaving is complete, remove the pins and weave in any ends. Place right sides together. Sew side edges together. If there are warp ends showing, you may wish to color them with paint or a felt-tip marker.

10. Finishing the body: Glue the body inside the tail section.

11. Upper body: Make two twisted cords from four 48" long strands of yarn (see page 45). Clamp one end to a solid surface, twist the other until you can't anymore. Put your index finger at the center of the cord, take the working end to the clamped end, and pinch together. Allow the cord to twist around itself. Tie a knot at the "frayed" end. Glue the spirals and twists to the upper body, covering the upper edge of the weaving.

Gluing the spirals and hair to the Mermaid.

12. Hair: Make four 6" long tassels (see page 14). Glue two to the front sides of her head and two to the back. Make another twisted cord the same as in Step 12. Glue and wrap the twisted cord around the top of her head, covering the tops of the tassels.

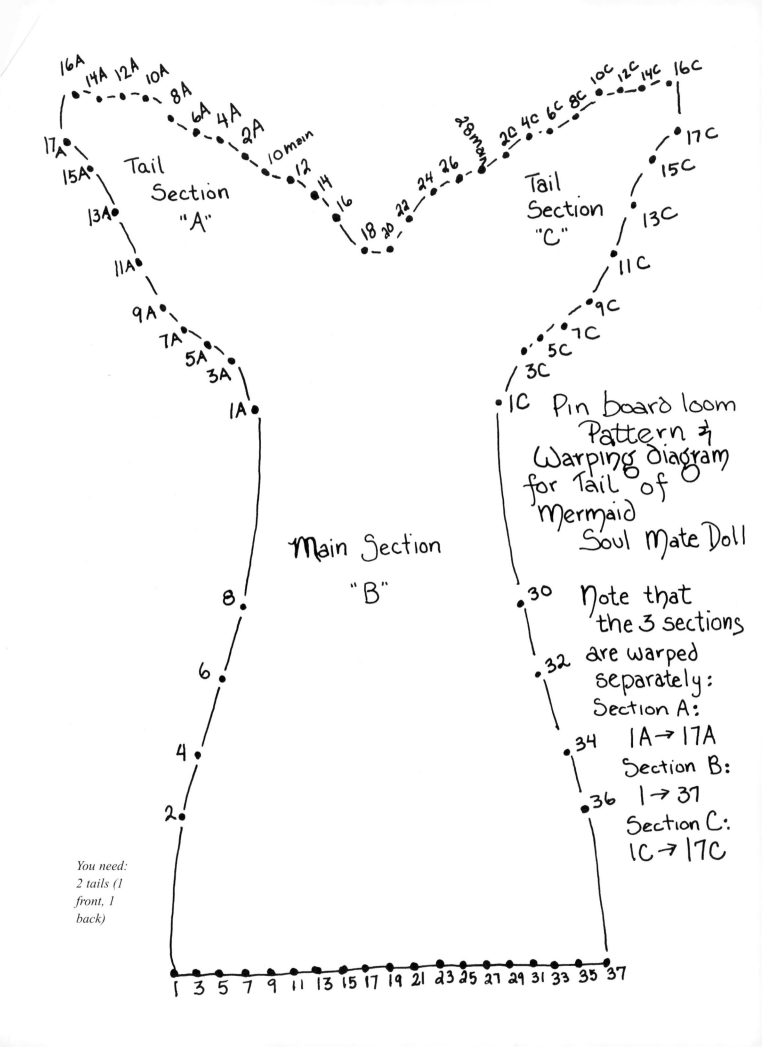

Determined Soul Mate Doll

I heard an author being interviewed. He was asked how his stories "happened." He said that a character would show up in his mind, and if it stuck around long enough, he would write a story about it. I was delighted to hear him say that, because dolls will frequently do the same thing to me.

That's the way it was with the Determined Soul Mate Doll. This little guy just kept showing up, insisting that he had to be in the book. "No," I told him firmly, "there's not enough room for you."

But the little monkey wouldn't give up. He kept insinuating himself into my designs and sketches, and finally I just had to give in. He makes me laugh, and every time I look at him, I remember his rather important message. He says, "When you want to achieve something, you've got to have insistence, persistence, and determination! And while you're at it, you might as well enjoy yourself!"

Materials and Tools

Yarn (approx. 2 oz.)*
Card stock
Paper clips (plastic-covered to
    match clothing color) or 18-
    gauge wire
Sharp craft knife
Cutting mat
Awl
Scissors
Wire snips
Acrylic paint and paint-
    brushes, colored pencils, or
    crayons
Glue
Hot glue gun and sticks
Small clamp
Needlenose pliers
6mm knitting needles
Darning needle
Row counter (paper and
    pencil will do)

*Used in this project: *Lily
Sugar'n Cream #76 Plum (pink
hat); Lily Sugar'n Cream #62
Emerald (green hat).*

1. Copy the pattern and glue it
to card stock. Note that there is
only one body section and two
of everything else.
2. Glue plain paper to back of
the card stock.
3. When dry, cut out and paint
both sides of the body, arms,
and legs.
4. To make the three joint wires,
bend one end from either the
paper clips or 1-1/2" lengths of
18-gauge wire. Pierce holes in
the doll parts at the dots with
the awl.

5. Slide one head section, the
body, and the other side of the
head onto one of the joint wires.
Before you bend the straight
end of the wire closed, run a
bead of glue inside of the head
from the mouth around the top
of the head to the center back
of the head. Close the loop.
Fold both loops firmly against
the head. Clamp the top of the
head until the glue dries.

Joining the head to the body.

6. Slide one of the join wires
into one arm, then the body, and
then the second arm. Close the
loop on the straight end. Fold
both ends firmly against the
body.

*Joining the arms. The head is glued
and clamped with a Victorian
Spring Clamp from Lee Valley
Tools.*

7. Slide the last joint wire into
the leg, then the body, and then
the second leg. Close the loop
on the straight end. Fold both
ends firmly against the body.

Joining the legs.

8. The hat is knitted on 6mm
knitting needles, using the
pattern for the Skater Soul Mate
Doll's hat (page 63).

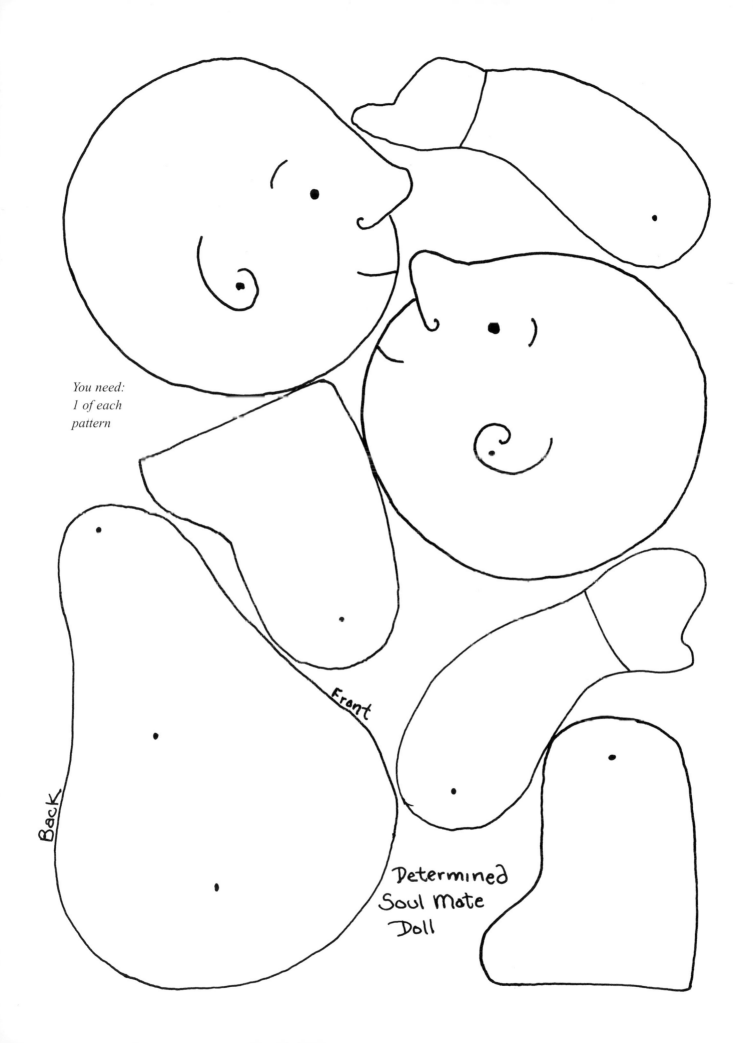

*You need:
1 of each
pattern*

Back

Front

Determined
Soul Mate
Doll

6 chapter

The Grandmothers

Over the last decade or so, we have become familiar with the concept of the "Inner Child." What we sometimes forget is that we also have an "Inner Teenager," an "Inner Mature Woman," and an "Inner Wise Old Woman."

I believe that we need to cultivate a relationship with that Inner Wise Old Woman, because she has so much wisdom to offer. She may not have all of the answers, but she sure knows how to ask a good question.

Recently, my family and I were watching the news. There was an item about the opening of a new arts center. An old woman from the audience was being interviewed. When asked her opinion, her eyes danced, and merrily she replied, "I'll be back tomorrow night!"

What a blessing she would be in an audience! Her zest and *joie de vivre* would infuse the audience with life. That would be a priceless gift to the performers! Moreover, what a gift to all of humanity to have a person of such warmth and enthusiasm among us!

What she was doing was to give "welcome" to the performers and the audience as well. One of the tasks of old age is to give welcome to the new. All children should be well and truly made welcome as they arrive in our arms. A child is, after all, the promise of the future.

Unfortunately, not all of us were given a proper welcome at our birth. Also, there can be people in our lives that make us feel most definitely *not* welcome. Ouch! The Welcome Soul Mate Doll is the embodiment of the loving welcome that we all deserve.

The Welcome Soul Mate Doll must be slightly open in order to be free standing.

Welcome Soul Mate Doll

Materials and Tools

Card stock
Paper: handmade, origami, gift
    wrap, etc.
Ribbons: 1/8" or 1/4" wide,
    approximately 7" long
Narrow lace: 1/4" to 1/2"
    wide, approximately 1" long
Skin-tone paper for face
Glue
Sharp craft knife and cutting
    mat
Permanent fine-point black
    marker
Scissors
Ruler
Colored pencils or watercolor
    paints
Optional: pin tool

1. Copy the pattern.
2. Glue decorative paper to the front and back of the card stock.

3. Trace the body shape onto the card stock. Cut out.
4. Trace the face onto skin-tone paper. Cut it out and glue to the body. Shade the face's features lightly with colored pencil to give them dimension. Color in the heart.
5. On right side of body, hold the ruler along each line AB and score both lines (run a pin tool or the dull side of a craft knife or scissors along the line).

Scoring line: AB.

Flip the doll over and score lines AC. Make sure that you press lightly when scoring. If you press too hard, it can split the fold.

Scoring line: AC.

6. Glue ribbons at sides of the face and lace across the fore-head.

Glue on the ribbon and lace around the face.

7. Fold the outside edges toward the center. Fold the arms down into a "welcome" position.

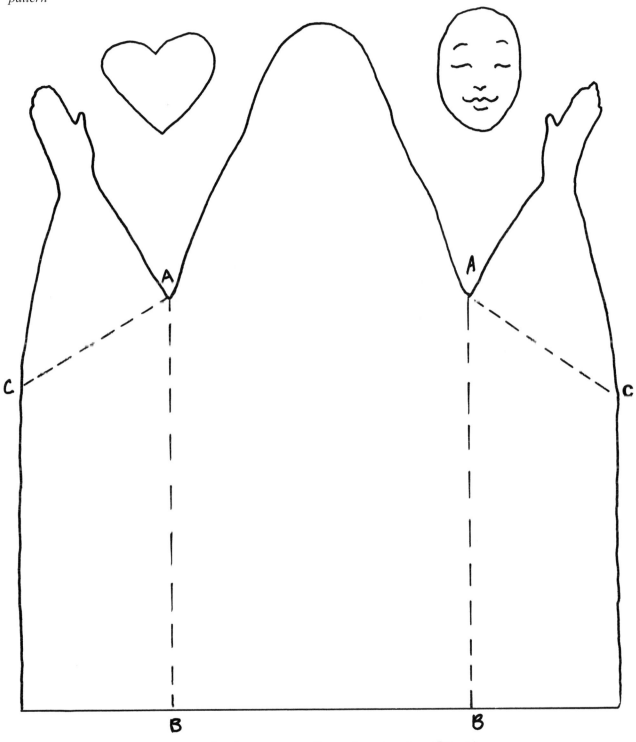

Welcome Soul Mate Doll
Score & fold on dotted lines

Millennium Soul Mate Doll

We are welcoming a new millennium, so making a Millennium Soul Mate Doll is a good way of celebrating it. What is a Millennium Soul Mate Doll? She's an expression of all that is positive, good, and true. She's the symbol of all the good stuff you want to invite into this new millennium, for the planet and all that's on it.

Materials and Tools

Sturdy card stock
Paper: handmade, origami, gift
  wrap, etc. (I drew on brown
  paper with a pen and brown
  ink)
Skin-tone paper for face and
  arms (or you can paint them)
Optional: ribbons, lace,
  charms, buttons, dried flow-
  ers, feathers, etc.
Glue
Paint and paintbrushes
Paper clips
Sharp craft knife and cutting
  mat
Permanent fine-point black
  marker
Scissors
Optional: hot glue gun and
  glue sticks
Ruler
Needlenose pliers
Wire snips
Colored pencils, inks, or
  watercolor or acrylic paints
Sharp darning needle or awl

1. Copy the patterns. Glue the main body, arms, skirt, and base pieces to card stock. Let dry completely.
2. Glue skin-tone paper to the other side of the arm pieces. When completely dry, cut them out.

The parts of the Millennium Soul Mate Doll.

3. Cut out the main body piece. Cut out the other upper body section and glue it to the back of the body. Glue paper to lower half of the body. (I like to tear the upper edge of this piece of paper and the lower edge of the second upper body pieces. This "feathers" the edge so that it blends in nicely.) Cut notches in both the skirt and body sections before you glue any decorative paper to the other side. Poke holes in the arm and shoulder sections.
4. Paint or color the dress or glue decorative paper to body front and back, shaping the neckline by cutting a pleasing neckline in the paper dress. Decorate both sides of the skirt and one side of the circular base with paint or ink.

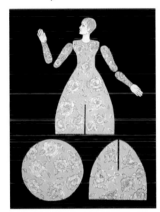

The Millennium Soul Mate Doll painted.

5. Arms: Straighten and cut two paper clips in half. Make the joints by forming a loop, bending it over, and inserting it through the hole at the elbow of the upper arm. Push it through the elbow hole of the lower arm. Twist the wire down to the arm, forming a loop, squeeze the loop over, and pinch it to make a snug pressure-fitted joint. Make another loop for the shoulder.

Push it through the hole at the shoulder in the body. Push the arm onto the wire. Twist the wire into the loop and squeeze shut. Repeat for other arm.
6. Paint hair.
7. Fit the body and skirt together, adjusting the notches as necessary. Place on the base; glue on if desired.

The Millennium Doll is a symbol of creating a positive future, but what if the present moment feels fraught?

In the midst, or aftermath, of a stressful day, we can feel as if we are a very small boat on a very large and stormy sea. More than anything, at that point, we need refuge: a harbor, a safe place to retreat to for a breather, for shelter and respite.

The Safe Harbor Soul Mate Doll symbolizes the feeling of being able to ride out the storm and to take deep pleasure in the fair weather. She says to us, "This, too, will pass, and you will learn from it."

The trick with taking refuge in the safe harbor is in learning when to venture out again. If, out of fear, we retreat too far into the safe harbor for too long, we will miss the boat. We will end up in stagnation, which can lead to an unlived life. That is a tremendous tragedy.

Knowing that we have a place of refuge gives us great resiliency and focus. It allows us to be courageous when it is time to venture out again.

In moments of stress, we can summon up the image of Safe Harbor. She's a good antidote to being washed out to sea by any unexpected waves of negativity.

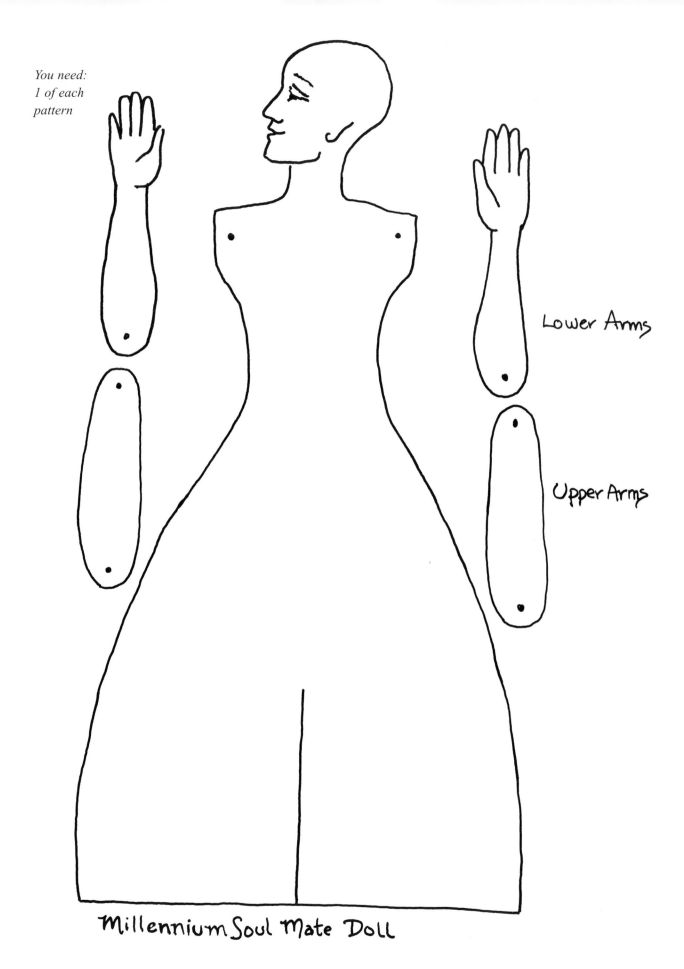

You need:
1 of each
pattern

Lower Arms

Upper Arms

Millennium Soul Mate Doll

Base - She just
sits on it. She's
not glued to it.

MillenniumSoul Mate Doll

Safe Harbor Soul Mate Doll

Materials and Tools

Card stock (lightweight is fine)
Closely-woven cotton for
  joints
Craft knife
Scissors
Paints, colored pencils, or
  crayons
Permanent black felt-tip
  marker

1. Copy the pattern. Glue the inside pattern to card stock. Let dry completely and cut out. Do not glue the outside sections of the doll to the card stock yet.
2. Cut two thin 1" by 3-1/2" fabric pieces. With the wrong sides of the doll up, line up the panels. Put a thin layer of glue on the fabric strips and center them on the joints between the center panel and two side panels (see pattern). The lower edges of the fabric strips are at the lower edge of the panels. Let dry completely.

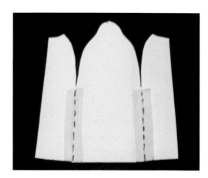

Making the hinges for the Safe Harbor Soul Mate Doll.

3. Cut out the outside sections of the doll. Glue them carefully to the outside of the card stock. Let dry completely.

4. Paint or color both the inside and outside of the doll. You could even write a poem or some other significant words inside her if you wish.

Painting the inside of the Safe Harbor Soul Mate Doll.

Speaking of courage, let me introduce the...

center edge

Safe Harbor Outside

Safe Harbor Soul Mate Doll Outside

center edge

Safe Harbor Outside

You need:
1 of each
pattern

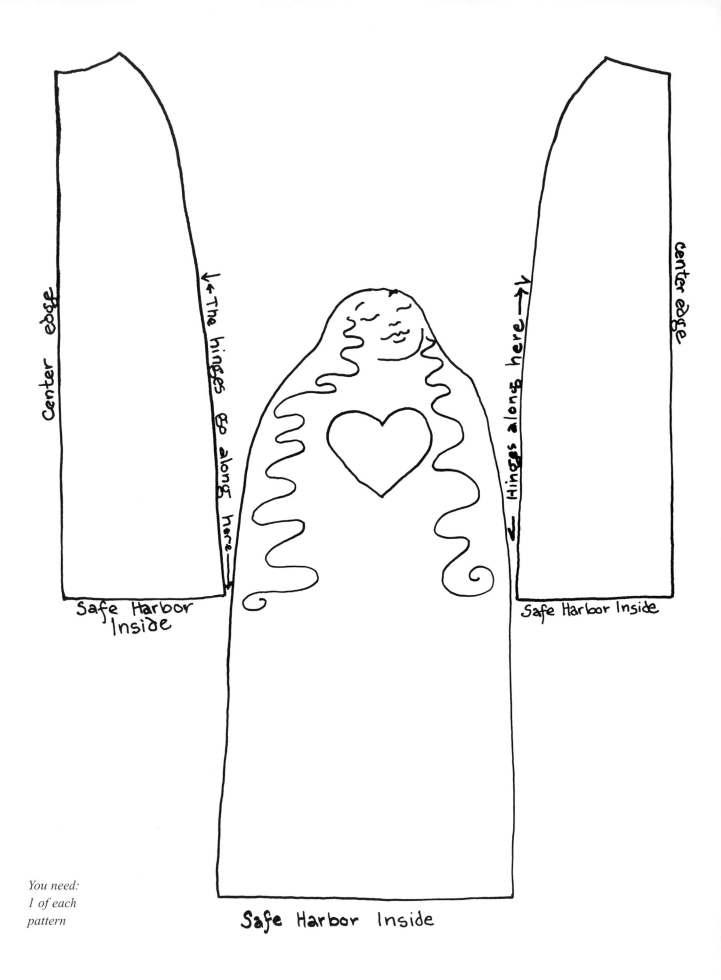

Center edge

← The hinges go along here →

Safe Harbor Inside

Hinges along here →

Center edge

Safe Harbor Inside

You need:
1 of each
pattern

Safe Harbor Inside

Ragged Edge Soul Mate Doll

Once, a friend told me about the theory of the "ragged edge," the point where the molecules in a metal are at their maximum state of excitation. Go past that point and the metal collapses or sheers. It's a dance of seeing how far an element can be pushed.

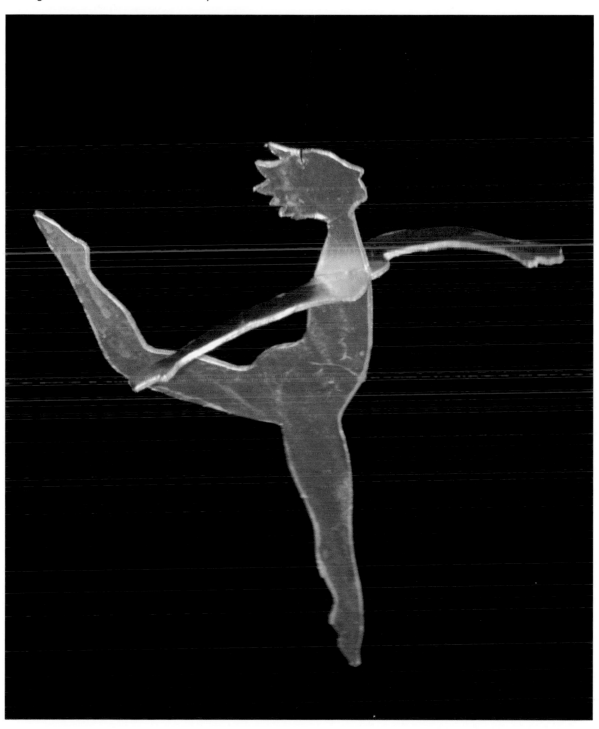

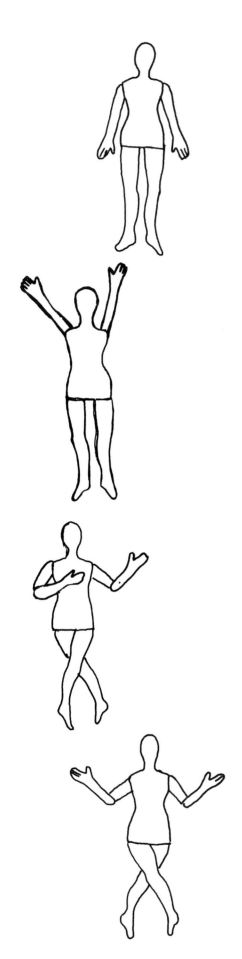

If one goes to the ragged edge in his or her life, he or she experiences a state of intense inspiration and rapture. You can't live there all of the time, because it would lead to madness or some other form of destruction. But, you can use moments at the ragged edge to infuse your life with passion, richness of expression, vigor, and zest.

The ragged edge is the leading edge of creativity. How do you get to the ragged edge of creativity? Certainly not by reckless or careless behavior. It takes enormous discipline and discernment to learn how to harness the intense energy of the ragged edge.

You need to dig in and discover what your passion is. By a passion, I mean the thing that brings you to your joy and truth. If you don't know, think about what brought you the greatest joy when you were a child. Your soul knew then what you were meant to be and do. These are things that wake us up and make us feel most alive. It is through our passions that we enhance and develop our creativity.

The Ragged Edge Soul Mate Doll is definitely not the antithesis of the Safe Harbor Soul Mate Doll. They dance together, not as polarized opposites, but as mutually respectful companions and fellow travelers.

She is made like the other interlocking Soul Mate Dolls (Soaring and Circle of Song, pages, 60 and 57 respectively. Remember to cut her notches and pierce the hanging hole

before gluing the paper on the second side. She is suspended by monofilament thread through the hole at the dot in her hair.

Materials and Tools

Gold wrapping paper or gold paint and a paintbrush
Card stock (because she is fairly small, lightweight card stock works fine)
Sharp craft knife
Cutting mat
Awl
Scissors
Glue
Hot glue gun and sticks
Monofilament thread

1. Copy the pattern and glue it to card stock.
2. Glue gold wrapping paper to the other side of the card stock. Let dry. (See Step 4 if you are painting the doll.)
3. Cut out doll. Pierce hole in hair.
4. Glue gold paper to the first side of the doll so that she is now gold on both sides. If you are painting her, paint both sides now. When the paint or glue is dry, cut out the doll pieces.
5. The notches are best if they fit together tightly, so cut them very narrow and keep checking for fit. When you are happy with the fit, run a line of hot glue along the underside of the arms at the join to seal them in place.
6. Thread monofilament through the hair. Make a loop at the other end and tie it in a knot so that you can hang up the doll.

Ragged Edge Soul Mate Doll

Grandmother Tree Soul Mate Doll

Trees are among the oldest living entities on our planet. We have much to be grateful to them for, including oxygen, food, medicine, shelter, the paper that gives us the ability to share ideas, the stabilizing force of their roots in the soil, and their shade.

Grandmother Tree understands death and interruption. She also understands enduring the wild winds of summer and the deep ice of winter. She is the embodiment of continuity.

Grandmother Tree is rooted in one place, so it would appear that she doesn't move. Yet, her roots reach deeper and deeper into the earth every year.

Her leaves dance constantly in the movement of the air. And when they finally let go of her, they race on the wind, leaving her far behind. When they finally come to rest, they carry her essence and bring nourishment to the place where they land. Grandmother Tree may stand still, but she reaches a long, long way. She is the symbol of wisdom and the ability to live with stark contrasts and uncertainty.

She is teeming with life, but you have to listen carefully to feel and hear it. In the winter, Grandmother Tree wears a lace shawl of glistening frost. I have her wear an antique lace scarf for her frosty veil. What would represent her lush foliage of summer?

(Refer to page 12 for Flat Soul Mate Doll templates.)

Materials and Tools

Bark*
11" by 17" piece of paper
Card stock
Wire
Yarn or raw wool
Optional: buttons, charms, etc.
Vintage lace
Sharp craft knife
Cutting mat
Hot glue gun and sticks

Scissors
Glue
Marking pen
Vanishing ink marker
Awl

*I used the bark from a deadfall tree for my Grandmother Tree Soul Mate Doll. The tree had died and been blown down in a wind storm. The bark lifted off easily. **Never, ever** strip bark from a living tree. If you don't have access to firewood that still has bark on it, or a tree that has died, there are other options: take a sheet of paper and a crayon and make a rubbing of the bark on a living tree, or find photographs of trees and copy them.*

1. Lay the template on the piece of paper. When drawing the body pattern for Grandmother Tree, instead of drawing legs, draw a trunk.

Drawing Grandmother Tree.

2. When I was drawing the head for the Grandmother Tree Doll that you see in the photographs, I tilted the head to one side. First, I drew her body, then tilted the template a little so that her head was now at an angle. The neck needed a little correction, so I used the vanishing ink marker for this until I was happy with the angle.

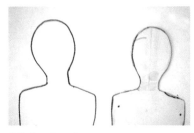

Tilt her head.

3. Experiment with her face, drawing it with vanishing ink marker until it's satisfying.
4. Glue the pattern to card stock. Cut out.
5. Glue the bark to the front and back of her "trunk," piecing as necessary.
6. Make elbow joints (page 13).
7. Make shoulder joints. Place the arms behind the doll's body when attaching the arms.
8. Glue on yarn or wool, or whatever appeals to you, for hair.
9. Glue on any desired embellishments.

And then, there's the...

Great Aunt Gardener Soul Mate Doll

You should have a Great Aunt Gardener in your life, even if you have to invent her!

She's the great aunt who made up her own rules as she went. She may have been the black sheep of the family, but she never let anyone pull the wool over her eyes!

She's a passionate one. Whatever she does, whether making a wedding cake, dancing the Flamenco, growing petunias, or building a stone wall, she does with gusto. Her garden is amazing to behold, and that's why she's called Great Aunt Gardener.

Great Aunt Gardener is often a diamond in the rough and is an incredible treasure. She reminds us to live our lives courageously, with zest, vigor, and enthusiasm. She is the epitome of energy, although she knows how to sit back and relax, too. Her motto is "Follow your own recipe and enjoy!"

An avocado pit may seem like an odd choice for creating a doll's head, but I really like the element of nature that comes from carving them. After all, Great Aunt Gardener is very connected to the natural world, and what could be more natural than using a seed for her head? Besides, it's neat to watch for the surprises in the drying and shrinking process. Not only that, but you can eat delicious guacamole while you're carving her!

An avocado pit is very easy to carve; it is moist and crisp. As it dries out, it darkens and shrinks, eventually looking like wood. When it is dried out, I like to rub off any little sawdusty bits with the end of a small dowel or bamboo skewer. It can be finished with a thin coat of glue, varnish, or oil or can be left unsealed or painted.

Materials and Tools for Doll's Head

Avocado pit
Embroidery floss* or sewing machine thread for hair
2 glass-head straight pins with black bead tops
5" long dowel, 1/12" in diameter or a bamboo skewer cut to 5", with one end sharpened
Sharp craft knife
Vanishing ink marker
Glue
Masking tape
Optional: oil or varnish
Hot glue gun and sticks
Scissors
Wire snips
Safety glasses (if you need to snip the points off the pins)

Note: Some of the items listed, like embroidery floss or thread, will be used when assembling the doll (see page 139).

*Used in this project: *One skein "Snow" opalescent embroidery floss from the Caron Collection. I also used a selection of many different colors of sewing machine thread held together as one strand to make her hair.*

1. Carefully peel the brown skin off the pit. It comes off more easily when the pit has dried in the air for a day or so. You can leave the pit for weeks before carving if you don't peel the skin off until just before you carve it.

Peel the avocado pit.

2. Choose which end of the pit will be her chin. Turn the pit so that the crack runs around the sides of the head. When it dries, it will separate slightly, so you don't want it running up the center of her face. Push the sharpened dowel into the base of the "skull," in back of the "chin." The dowel is going to be the neck and spine, so you want it going into the avocado pit head at the right place. Tilting the pit before pushing the dowel in gives her an interesting expression.

3. With the vanishing ink marker, draw a vertical line up the center of the face. Draw a

After inserting the dowel, draw reference lines.

horizontal line at the center of the face. This is where the eyes will be drawn. Draw a second line halfway between the first line and the chin. The nostrils will sit on this line. Draw a wedge-shaped nose from the second line up to the eye line and two eyebrow lines.

4. With the sharp craft knife, cut straight down along the nose lines and along the eyebrow line. Carve away a layer of the pit, so that the nose, cheekbones, and eyebrows are now about 1/8" higher than the rest of the face around them.

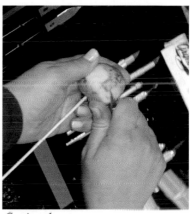
Cutting the nose.

5. Draw a third line halfway between the second line and the chin. This is where the mouth will be.

6. Draw two dots for the eyes on the first horizontal line. Draw

Working on the eyes and mouth.

two lines around each eye dot for the eyelids.

7. Cut little wedges away from the eye sockets to form the forehead.

Working on the eye socket.

8. Cut away little bits under the eyes to shape the eye socket and cheek bones.

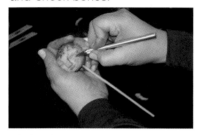

Under the eyes.

9. Shave down the eyelids a little. Cut a line across the center of the eyelids for the opening. Push a black beadhead straight pin into the center of each eye. This opens the lids. Use the end of the dowel to push the pins in as far as possible.

Pushing the pins in to form the eyes.

10. Cut a curving line for her smile. Her lips are above and below this line. Shave away tiny wedges above and below the lip to shape them. Shave away little bits along the mouth line to open her smile up a little.

Nipping away at the mouth.

11. Keep nipping and shaving away tiny wedges. Shape the features by taking tiny cuts. Widen her smile by nipping out wedges in her cheeks. Emphasize laughter lines and dimples.

Making dimples.

12. Give her a double chin by carving out around her chin.

Working on the chin.

13. Keep turning the head from side to side and up and down. You need to see the head from all sides. Remember that the face is not flat on the front, but wraps around the head.

Keep turning the head in all directions.

14. Let her head dry out completely. It will take several days, depending on the humidity in your area.

15. After she is all dried out, you may need to adjust little oddities that appear in the drying stages. It is still quite easy to carve the pit even after it has dried. As the avocado pit dries out, it shrinks, so you may need to push the pins in a little further. If the points emerge on the other side of the head, put on safety glasses and carefully snip the sharp pin points off with wire snips.

16. If the crack opens up too wide in the pit after the head has dried out, dribble some glue into it. You might need a little masking tape to keep the glue in the crack.

While you are waiting for her head to dry, you can make her clothes and accessories.

Materials and Tools

Sturdy piece of foam, or ceiling tile, wrapped in plastic wrap and taped, about 8-1/2" by 11"
Yarn or embroidery floss
7" of 1-1/2" wide ribbon
Small amount of stuffing
Pins
Scissors
Darning needle
Optional: small knitting needle or a narrow, small ruler
Hot glue gun and glue sticks

Used in this project: ⁺Striped coat: Bernat Cot'n Soft, one ball "Bumbleberry" (1.5 oz); Solid coat: Bernat Chenille, one ball "Frosted Blue" (1.6 oz); Watercolours by Caron, four skeins Evergreen and one skein Wildberries.

Preparing to Weave

1. Copy the pattern for the woven coat for the pin board loom (page 24) (one sleeve and one coat body panel).
2. Place the pattern on the piece of foam or tile and insert pins at each dot. Tie the warp to pin #1 and follow the numbered sequence to the last pin.
3. Weave two sleeves and four body sections, two for the front and two for the back. (You can weave a fifth body section in a contrasting color for the front of the undergarment instead of using ribbon if you wish).

Weaving

1. When weaving the front and back sections of the coat, you will weave up to pin #4 and 18 and then remove them. You will then weave to the top of the piece. When you reach the top, snip the weft yarn, weave in the ends, and gently pull the pins out.
2. Insert the pins into the same holes and weave the next piece.
3. If you want to weave a collar for the coat, set up a pin board loom to make a 2" square (see the Forgiveness Fairy Doll, page 91). Weave a 2" square and fold it in half diagonally, gluing it on after the coat is glued in place on doll.

Assembling Coat

1. Sew the center back seam.
2. Sew the shoulder seams, joining the two front pieces to the back. Leave the center front open.

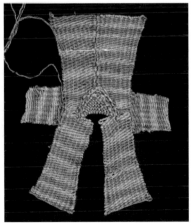

Sew the center back seam and shoulder seams of the pin board woven coat for Great Aunt Gardener.

3. Fold the sleeve in half to find the center. Pin the center to the shoulder seam. Sew the sleeve to the side edge of the coat.
4. Sew the underarm seams of the sleeve and the coat's side seams.

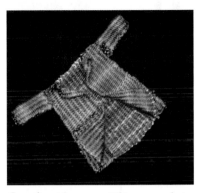

Sew the side seams. This example is shown with a contrasting front panel inserted.

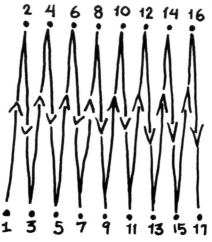

2 4 6 8 10 12 14 16

1 3 5 7 9 11 13 15 17

Warping Diagram: Sleeve

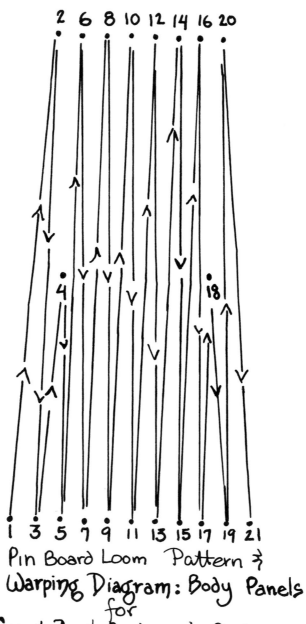

2 6 8 10 12 14 16 20

4   18

1 3 5 7 9 11 13 15 17 19 21

Pin Board Loom Pattern ≩
Warping Diagram: Body Panels
for
Great Aunt Gardener's Coat
Insert pins in board at numbered
dots to make pin board loom

Instead of the coat, you may prefer to make her a paper kimono (shown on the doll at left on page 130).

Materials and Tools

Paper: brown, handmade, origami, or other decorative paper
Small square of scrap paper
Glue
Vanishing ink marker
Scissors
Ruler

1. To make a full-sized pattern for the kimono, trace the pattern in the book and lay it on a folded piece of paper. Transfer the folding and cutting lines to both halves of your pattern. Note that the fold line at the center back of the pattern is not a fold line when making the box pleat at the back of the kimono.
2. With the vanishing ink marker, copy the outline of the pattern onto the kimono paper. Because this kimono is made in paper, there is no seam allowance.

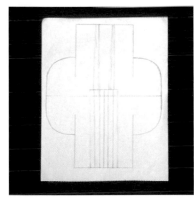

The kimono is drawn.

3. With the vanishing ink marker or a pencil and ruler, draw the cutting lines at the center front of the kimono, neck back, and sleeve slashes.

4. With the vanishing ink marker and a ruler, draw the fold lines for the lapels on the front, the dart on the back, and the shoulder fold lines. Notice that the lapels extend over the shoulder fold to the back of the kimono
5. Cut out the kimono and the cutting lines at center front, neck back, and sleeve slashes. Optional: Scrunch the paper up a few times to distress it before cutting the openings.
6. Make a box pleat in the back of the kimono. With the right side up, fold the wrong side of the kimono together along the two lines that are closest to the center back. Now, fold along each of the other two lines to make a tuck; the right sides come together under the center back panel, which is the box pleat. Glue the small piece of paper on the inside of the kimono, at the top of the box pleat, to hold it in place.

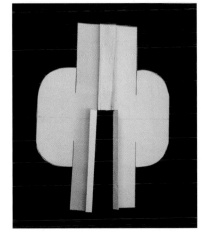

The box pleat folded in the back and the lapels folded in the front.

7. Making the lapels: With the right side up, fold the center section toward the sides twice.
8. Fold the kimono in half at the horizontal shoulder line.

The kimono folded at the shoulders. Part of the lapels extends over the shoulders to the back.

9. Glue the side seams and the lower edge of the sleeve. Leave the underarm slashes unglued.

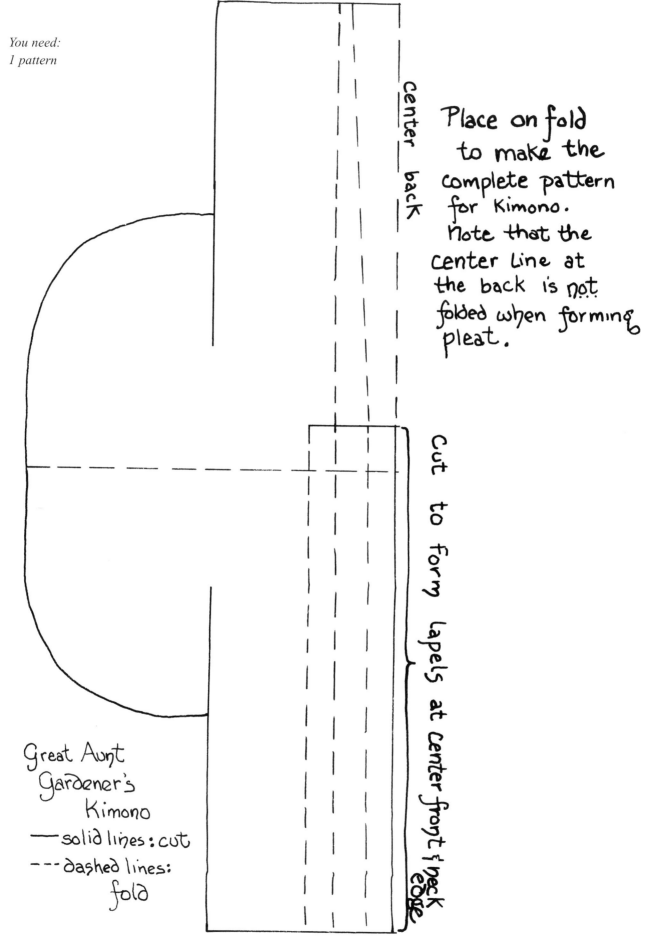

You need:
1 pattern

center back

Place on fold
to make the
complete pattern
for Kimono.
Note that the
center Line at
the back is not
folded when forming
pleat.

Cut to form lapels at center front & neck edge

Great Aunt
Gardener's
Kimono
—— solid lines: cut
- - - dashed lines:
fold

Crocheted Hat

Follow the Basic Crocheted Hat Pattern on page 15. I made the striped hat with Bernat Cot'n Soft "Bumbleberry" with a 3.5mm (E, 4) crochet hook. I made the solid color hat with two strands of Bernat Embroidery Floss (C1 Pastels, soft gray) and a 3.5mm (E, 4) crochet hook.

Crocheted Baskets

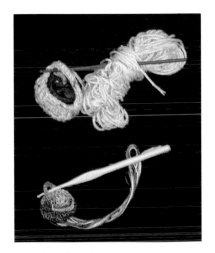

Crocheted baskets.

I made the larger basket with Bernat Sugar'n Cream #101 Moss Lagoon, with a 3.5mm (E, 4) crochet hook. I made the smaller basket with Bernat Embroidery Floss C3, Ombres, Brown. (You can make both the large and small basket with these directions.)

Ch 3. Join to form a ring.
R. 1: Ch 3, 11 dc in ring. Join to top of ch 3. [12 dc]
R. 2: Ch 3, 1 dc in base of ch 3, 2 dc in each of next 11 dc. Join to ch 3. [24 dc]
R. 3: Ch 3, 1 dc in each dc. Join to ch 3. [24 dc]
R. 4: Ch 1, sl st in each dc. Join. [24 sl st]
R. 5: Ch 15, skip 12 st and join to other side of basket.
R. 6: Ch 1, sl st in each ch across. Join to first side of basket. Cut thread, weave in ends.

Vest

To make her vest (shown on the doll at right on page 130), see the instructions for the Gatekeeper's Vest, page 32. I worked the vest with a three-strand Igolochkoy embroidery needle and Wildflowers Nefertiti, Midnight, and Antica AT7 from the Caron collection. You may choose to needlepoint the vest or use your favorite style of embroidery.

You need:
1 pattern

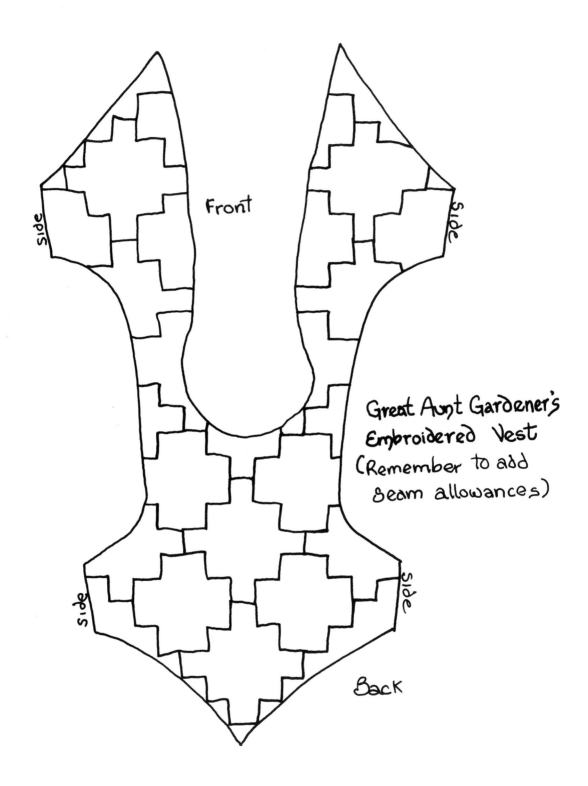

Front

side

side

Great Aunt Gardener's
Embroidered Vest
(Remember to add
seam allowances)

side

side

Back

(When head is completely dry.)

Materials and Tools for Optional Glasses

Piece of wire approximately 3"
   long or straighten out a large
   plastic-covered paper clip
Wire snips
Needlenose pliers
Hot glue gun and sticks
Small dowel, paintbrush, or
   pen

Note: See page 131 for additional items needed.

1. About 1" from one end, wrap the wire or straightened paper clip around a dowel, paintbrush, or pen for the first lens. Pull the object out and check where to place the second lens by holding it up to her face. Wrap the wire around the object again, pull it out, and you've got glasses. Bend the arms of the glasses to fit her face. Trim off any extra wire and glue the ends to the sides of her head.

Making her glasses.

2. Copy the body and hand patterns and glue them to card stock. Cut them out. Interlock the body and base sections at the notches. Run a bead of glue along the notches.

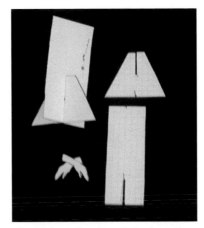

Great Aunt Gardener's body and hands.

3. Hair: I used only a few inches of embroidery floss for each head. Lay a 4" strand of thread or crochet cotton along your left (if you are right handed) index finger. Wrap embroidery thread around your index finger ten times. You have wrapped it over the crochet cotton, so now tie the crochet cotton into a knot.

Making her bangs with a tassel.

Slip it off your finger and snip the bottom of the loops. Make three of these hair "tassels." Glue one to the top of her head to make bangs.

4. Glue the hat to her head. Now, glue one hair tassel to each side of her face, tucking the top of the tassel up inside the hat. Trim any loose ends on hair.

5. Glue the neck stick with the head to the back of the body, being sure to leave about 1/2" of stick between her head and body for the neck.

Glue on her hat and glue tassels at the sides.

Glue head to the body.

6. Put the kimono or coat on her body: Mark the center of a chenille stem (fold it in half and put a dot of ink on it). Slip it inside the kimono or coat, in front of the body armature. The chenille stem goes out through the sleeves. Fold it back up inside the sleeves, making sure that it is slightly shorter than the sleeves. Glue the center of the stem to the center front of the body, approximately 1/2" from the top edge of the body. Glue hands to the chenille stems and to inside of the sleeves.

Put the coat on the body. You might need to trim the body if the coat doesn't fit the way you want it to. The chenille stem is in and the hands are glued on.

7. Put a small dab of glue on the bottom of the back base and glue the hem of coat or kimono to the base.

8. Ignore if you are using the kimono: Turn lapels down on the upper edges of the coat. Glue in place.

9. Glue the fifth woven panel inside the front of coat or kimono, or fold under a 1/2" hem at the top of the ribbon. Glue it under her chin, wrapping it partially around her neck. Slip it inside the coat front. Glue the inside edges of the kimono or coat front to the edges of ribbon or panel, so that it shows. Turn up the hem of ribbon to match the kimono or coat hem. The panel doesn't need to be turned up. Glue it in place.

Glue in the ribbon or woven front panel.

10. Tuck a little stuffing up her front, above the base. Put a dab of glue on the front of the body base and glue the center front of the ribbon or panel to the body.

11. Slip the vest on. You may need to snip the slashes in the underarms of the kimono a little to get the vest on.

12. Bend the hands a little and put the small basket in her hand.

You need:
1 of each
pattern

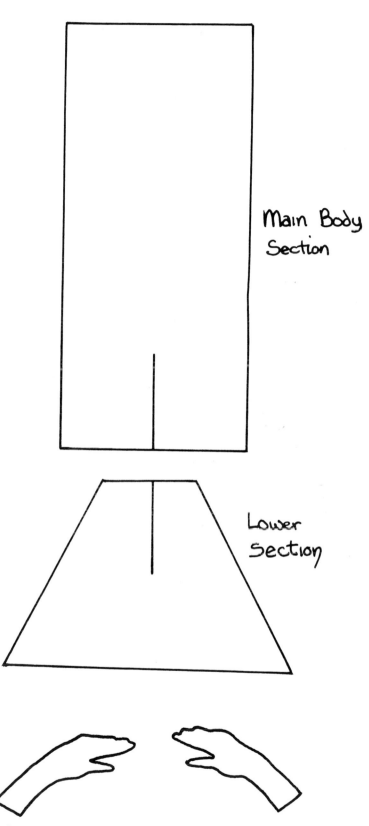

Main Body
Section

Lower
Section

Great Aunt Gardener: Body & Hands

conclusion

I believe that we are meant to live our lives joyously, richly, authentically, and energetically, finding in and around us the fullest expression of the delightful, beautiful, and wonder-filled world that we can. That takes commitment, energy, and courage. We need to give ourselves permission to live so fully. It sometimes means that we have to go deep into the woods, whatever that means for you. Mollie Whuppie did it, and you can, too.

I hope the Soul Mate Dolls have brought some useful and pleasing new threads into the tapestry of life that you are weaving yourself. May they open new doorways for you on the journey to creativity, healing, and wholeness.

I hope that Soul Mate Dolls will open doorways to creativity, healing, and wholeness for you.

glossary

AWL: A sharp tool that is specially designed for piercing holes—very handy!

BASEBALL STITCH: Have you ever noticed how a baseball is sewn together? The edges of the pieces butt up against each other and are held in place with stitches that slant together, forming a "V." This is a great way to sew woven, knitted, or crocheted pieces together. The needle comes up from the wrong side of the pieces to be joined, goes down into the space between them, and comes up from the wrong side of the other piece. This forms the slanted stitch and is repeated until the two pieces are completely sewn together.

CARD STOCK AND CARDBOARD: Card stock is layers of paper bonded together to make a sturdy product. Cereal boxes and pantyhose packages are made of card stock. Cardboard is made up of three layers of paper or card stock. They are bonded into a sandwich that has a layer or waves (corrugations) between two flat layers.

METAPHOR: A word picture that helps form a bridge to new understanding. Metaphors help us make creative leaps. It means "more than"; most metaphors are truly greater than the sum of their parts.

PIN TOOL: If you stuck a darning needle into a craft knife handle you would have a pin tool. Why would you do such a thing? Because it's a handy tool for scoring folds, helping to turn small sewn pieces right side out, scratching designs into paint- or crayon-covered surfaces, and many other little odd jobs.

SCORE: When you score a fold, you run a pin tool, the dull side of a table knife, or the dull edge of a pair of scissors along a line that you want to fold smoothly. This compresses the fibers of the paper so that they fold exactly where you want them to. Just don't press too hard or you can cut the line instead of scoring it.

SHED: This is the space between one set of warp strands and the other set when you are weaving. You start by aiming in one direction, let's say from the right to left. You go over, and then under, alternate warp strands across the row. This is one shed. When you are weaving the next row, from the left to the right, you'll be going under the warps that you went over in the last row, and over the ones that you went under. This is your second shed.

SHED STICK: To speed up the weaving process, you can weave a small knitting needle or narrow ruler into one of the sheds. Once you have woven the shed stick into the weaving, you can leave it there. It slides to the top of the warp strands, and when you have to weave the row that it opens, you lift up on it and slide the needle or shuttle into the space that it makes between the warp strands. You will still have to go over/under/across for the other shed, but you'll find it much quicker not to go over/under on both rows.

SOUMAK STITCH: Soumak is a good way to start and end woven pieces. You pass the weft over two warp strands and go back under one warp strand. This is repeated all the way across the row.

SQUARE KNOT: This is a knot that's very handy for joining threads in weaving. Go right end over left end and under, left end over right end and through the loop; pull up.

VANISHING INK MARKERS: These are some of my favorite tools. They have purple ink that disappears a day or so after you draw the line. Better yet, they also come with a white end that erases the marks. I use them to draw things like preliminary doll faces, because they don't mess up the paper the way pencils and erasers do. They are available in the notion's department of sewing stores.

WARP: Warp strands are the lengthwise strands of yarn, floss, or string that you weave on. They are the foundation of the woven piece, providing the strength of the finished piece. Usually, smooth, strong yarns are chosen to be warp.

WEFT: Weft strands are the horizontal yarns that go in and out of the warp strands. Weft can be very decorative and doesn't have to be particularly strong. All kinds of things can be used as weft besides yarn, floss, and string, including fabric strips, feathers, strips of plastic, unspun wool, or whatever you can dream up!

suppliers & sources

Bernat/Spinrite (including Lily brand) yarns were used throughout the book. They are widely available at your favorite local yarn store.

Birdhouse Enterprises
4438 G Street
Sacramento, CA 95819
Phone: 916-452-5212
Fax: 916-452-1212
Igolochkoy Embroidery Needles and packages (not individual ones) of charms.

Buxton Brook Designs
1382 W. Main St.
Williamstown, MA 01267
Phone and fax: 413-458-2782
I am so excited that these beautifully crafted little looms are available again! They come in sets of two looms. There is a 2" square and a 4" square; the rectangles are 2" by 4" and 4" by 6".

The Caron Collection
55 Old South Avenue
Stratford, CT 06615
Phone: 800-862-2766
Fax: 203-381-9003
E-mail: mail@caron-net.com
Hand-dyed embroidery threads

Harrisville Designs
P.O. Box 806, Center Village
Harrisville, NH 03450
Phone: 800-338-9415
Fax: 603-827-3335
The Lap Loom A. While you are ordering this wonderful loom, order an extra shuttle and their nifty shed opening device, The Wonder Wand.

Lacis
3163 Adeline Street
Berkeley, CA 94703
Phone: 510-843-7178
Fax: 510-843-5018
E-mail: staff@lacis.com
Lacis Square Loom

My favorite source for tools and fine hardware is **Lee Valley Tools Ltd.**
In Canada:
Lee Valley Tools Ltd.
P.O. Box 6295, Station J
Ottawa ON K2A 1T4
Phone: 800-267-8767

In the USA:
Lee Valley Tools Ltd.
P.O. Box 1780
Ogdenburg, NY 13669
Phone: 800-871-8158